COLORFUL
GLASSCRAFTING

By Jos H. Eppens-van Veen

STERLING PUBLISHING CO., INC. NEW YORK

Oak Tree Press Co., Ltd. London & Sydney

OTHER BOOKS OF INTEREST

Ceramic Creations
Ceramics—and How to Decorate Them
Creative Claywork
Creative Enamelling & Jewelry-Making
Enamel without Heat
Etching (and other Intaglio Techniques)
Lacquer & Crackle
Make Your Own Elegant Jewelry

Making Mosaics
Metal and Wire Sculpture
Nail Sculpture
Practical Encyclopedia of Crafts
Prints—from Linoblocks and Woodcuts
Stained Glass Crafting
Tin-Can Crafting
Tole Painting

Translated by Manly Banister
Adapted by Anne E. Kallem

Sources of Glass Supplies and Equipment

In United States:

Thomas Thompson Co.
1539 Old Deerfield Road
Highland Park, Illinois 60035

Stains

Blue Grass Art and Hobby Center
Box 206
Blue Grass, Iowa

Kay Kinney Contour Glass
725 Broadway
Laguna Beach, California 92651

J & H Art Glass Supply Co.
522 Madison
Fredonia, Kansas 66736

Stained Glass

Blenko Glass Co.
Milton, West Virginia 25341

Conniek Studios
9 Harcourt Street
Boston, Massachusetts 02116

In England:

Berlyne-Bailey and Company Ltd.
29 Smedley Lane
Cheetham, Manchester M8 8XB

Copyright © 1973 by Sterling Publishing Co., Inc.
419 Park Avenue South, New York, N.Y. 10016
British edition published by Oak Tree Press Co., Ltd., Nassau, Bahamas
Distributed in Australia and New Zealand by Oak Tree Press Co., Ltd.,
P.O. Box 34, Brickfield Hill, Sydney 2000, N.S.W.
Distributed in the United Kingdom and elsewhere in the British Commonwealth
by Ward Lock Ltd., 116 Baker Street, London W 1
The original edition was published in The Netherlands under the title, "Spelen met Glas,"
© 1970 by Unieboek N.V., Bussum, Holland
Manufactured in the United States of America
All rights reserved
Library of Congress Catalog Card No.: 72–81044
ISBN 0-8069-5226–1   UK 7061 2382 4
5227–X

CONTENTS

BEFORE YOU BEGIN

A New Method of Working Glass

Glass bending is not new. Even the early Romans did it. *Coloring window glass and then bending it, however, is a new process.* Only a short time ago a new product was developed for coloring window glass. If you know something about glass you may think: All you need is stained glass, the kind used to make panels with lead strips! Such stained glass sheets are often decorated with designs applied with dark glass paint. There are also available colored glass paints for painting colors on colorless glass. However, most of these paints tend to lose their color when the temperature is raised high enough to cause the glass to soften. And that is what you are going to do—soften glass just enough to bend it or to make two pieces of glass stick together, so that you can melt connecting links between them for pieces of jewelry and to make wall collages and plaques in which many kinds of fire-resistant materials are melted in between glass plates. You will also make colored dishes and ashtrays that look a great deal different from the ones you see year in and year out—in short, dishes with great style and beauty.

The new glass-coloring material is called Glas-O-Past-X. It suffers no loss of color when heated to a high temperature. It is an oil paint, available in tubes and can be thinned with turpentine or paint thinner. There are transparent as well as opaque colors. With the exception of red, all colors of the same kind can be mixed together. White can also be mixed with transparent colors to produce a pretty, opaline tint.

The Properties of Glass

Like ice, glass is a congealed fluid. It is a poor conductor of heat and has a very high coefficient of expansion. (This means that glass expands considerably when heated.) Whenever you work with glass, you make use of one of its most important properties—its ability to stick to other glass at a temperature far under the melting point of the material. This makes it possible to enclose, for decorative purposes, certain heat-resistant materials between two glass plates, which is commonly called "lamination." Glass not only sticks to glass, but to other materials as well, such as, for example, to earthenware or to a kiln shelf! To keep glass from sticking to a kiln shelf, you will have to apply a resistant coating, or "separator," to the latter to keep the glass from sticking when it is heated. Separators are available at all craft shops.

It is not possible to provide an *exact* softening temperature, as that is determined by both the thickness and the composition of the glass being heated. The softening temperature of window glass, however, in double-strength thickness, lies between 1420° F. (771° C.) and 1470° F. (799° C.).

Single-strength glass has a somewhat higher softening temperature; it is harder as it must offer more resistance to pressure. (Single-strength glass is $\frac{1}{16}''$ thick; double-strength glass

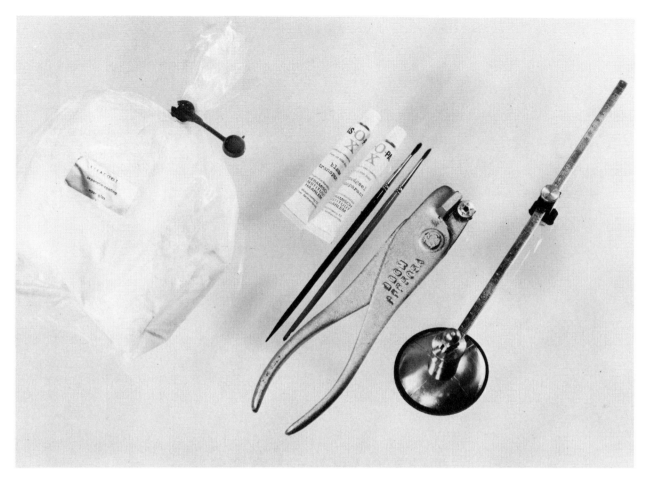

Illus. 1. Plain window glass can be transformed into beautifully colored bowls, dishes, mobiles, plaques, or any number of other objects with these simple materials—kiln separator, Glas-O-Past-X, brushes, combination glass-cutter-pliers, and a glass-circle cutter.

is $\frac{1}{8}''$ thick.) The very thin glass used in picture framing, called picture glass, is still harder and has a still higher softening temperature. Since there is no precise way of telling exactly what the softening temperature of a given piece of glass is, you will have to make use of a "guessing gauge"—the color of the cut edge of the glass. Glass that has a softening temperature of 1420° to 1470° F. (771° to 799° C.) displays a pronounced green color when you look at it edge-on.

You will not use any kind of colored, or "stained," glass in your work. Such glass is colored through and through with colored oxides, and different colors have widely divergent softening temperatures. This means that one kind of colored glass may not reach its softening temperature until another kind is completely melted, which would ruin your kiln shelves and forming equipment. This can never happen, however, with uncolored glass. Colored bottles are the only exception, and these you will work with later on.

After heating, glass must have an opportunity to relieve the strains that have been set up in it by cooling slowly. After you have turned off the kiln, you must not open it for at least 24 hours, until the kiln and everything in it has cooled to the temperature of the surroundings. If you open the kiln too soon and cold air strikes the hot glass, it is likely to crack or shatter.

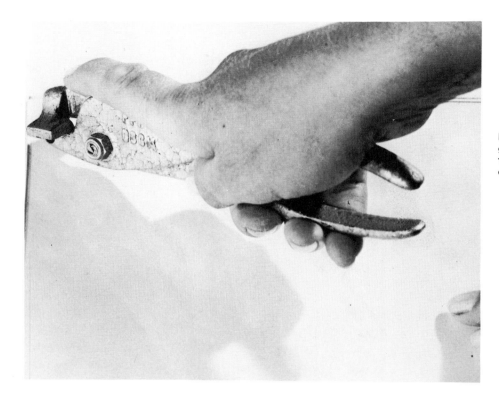

CUTTING GLASS

We always speak of "cutting" glass, though this is the wrong term, since glass cannot be cut. What you do in cutting glass is to first score the polished surface with a scratched line. This line guides the *breaking* of the glass. Use a narrow, $\frac{3}{4}$"-thick smooth-edged board for a straight-edge. For cutting glass, use a combination glass cutter and pair of glass-breaking pliers. If you cannot locate the combination tool, you can purchase a glass cutter and a pair of glass pliers separately at a glass supply house.

Practice cutting on a large piece of waste glass. Just about any glass shop or hardware dealer who handles glass will give you waste pieces without charge. It is wise to have your first round glass plates cut where you buy the glass and ask to watch while it is being done. That way, you will see how it is done. At the same time, you can take advantage of the situation and ask for some waste glass. The glass man will probably be glad to have you take it—it will save him the trouble of throwing it away. You can make good use of all kinds of waste glass—single-strength glass, double-strength glass, plate glass, shop-window glass, textured glass, milk glass, ground glass, corrugated frosted glass, in short, all the kinds of glass that a glass supply house can offer. A good place to keep your stock of glass plates is in a phonograph-record rack. Arrange the glass in the slots according to size, thickness, and so on, so that you will not have to pick over the whole pile of glass every time you want a certain piece. (Also, save all medicine bottles, mustard jars, face-cream jars, glass jugs, soda, wine, and beer bottles, jam and instant coffee jars.)

Now, from a large piece, cut a number of smaller pieces all alike. Here is how to do it: Draw straight lines the desired distance apart on a piece of white paper and place this under the piece of glass. Lay the straight-edge along the first line and hold it down firmly. Dip the glass cutter in turpentine or kerosene to lubricate it, hold it in a nearly horizontal position tight against the straight-edge, and draw it towards you in a single movement, so that it leaves a scratch behind it on the surface of the glass. Do not press down heavily on the cutter, for, if you do, the surface of the break will not be smooth. You should not hear a grainy or scratchy noise from the point. It should be more of a whispering sound that goes "szooff."

Grip the glass with the combination pliers in such a way that the glass cutter is down and the scored side of the glass is up, and snap the glass off along the scored line. A quick movement does it. The glass will break exactly along the scored line without damage to your hands. If it does not do this, and the break goes awry, it is probably because you did not hold the glass exactly square in the pliers, so that the pressure was not equal on both sides. After practicing a few times, you will be able to snip off glass with the pliers as if you were cutting paper.

You can cut glass in not-too-sharp S-curves as well as in straight lines. You can also cut out leaf shapes, with sharp points sticking out on both sides. It is not possible, however, to cut a sharp angle, because the break always runs the length of the scored line. S-shapes are cut far better and easier with glass pliers than with a separate glass cutter, because the pliers are easier to handle. (See Illus. 4.)

In order to make round plates, you will need a glass-circle cutter. This consists of a cutter-holder provided with a rubber suction cup which can be fastened securely to the

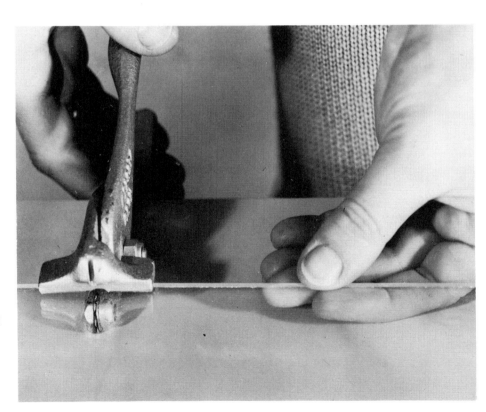

Illus. 3. Snapping the glass along the scored line.

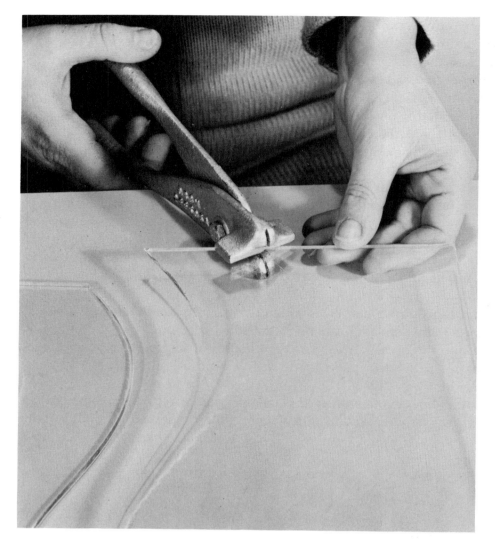

Illus. 4. Not-too-sharp S-curves are easy to cut with the glass pliers.

face of the glass. The holder serves as an axis around which rotates a measuring bar which has the glass cutter fastened to it. The cutter is adjustable on the bar so that you can set it for any desired radius of circle.

To learn to cut glass circles, begin with double-strength window glass and start with large circles. Cutting small circles is more difficult than cutting large ones.

Take a square piece of paper and a sheet of glass the same size (8″ or 10″ square). Draw both diagonals from corner to corner on the paper and lay this under the glass. By making use of the guide lines on the paper, you will find it easy to position exactly the glass-circle cutter on the square of glass. By pulling the handle on top of the holder to one side, you expel the air from the suction cup and firmly secure the cutting device. Now, adjust the cutter on the bar so that the point touches the glass ⅜″ in from the side of the square. Take a large wad of cotton, soak it in paint thinner, and turn it full circle round the glass, guiding it with the cutter, and taking care that the cutting point does not touch the glass.

8

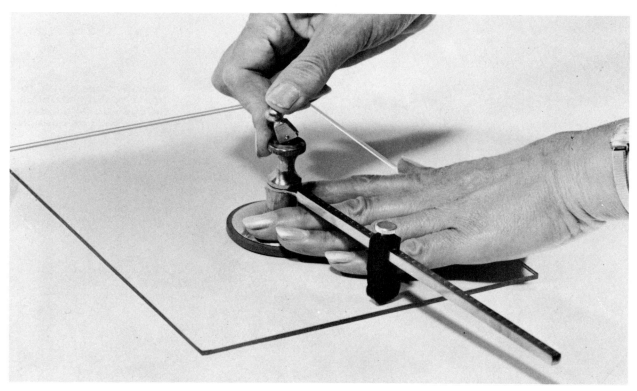

Illus. 5. When using the glass-circle cutter, pull the little handle on top to one side to release air from the suction cup so it will grip the glass firmly.

Illus. 6. Before scoring the surface with the glass-circle cutter, you must lubricate it with paint thinner.

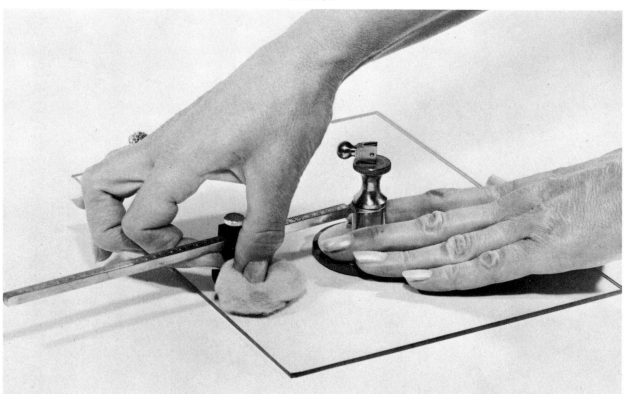

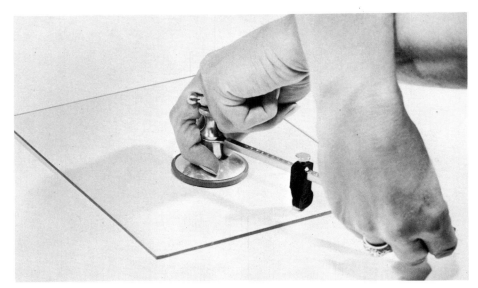

Illus. 7. Your aim is to make a complete circle in one stroke, so start as far back as possible.

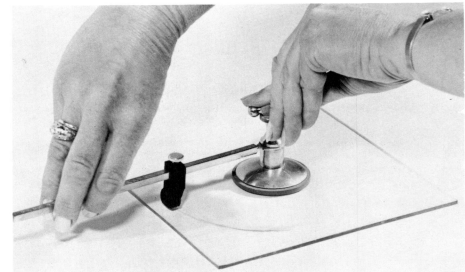

Illus. 8. Then, make a single quick scoring. This will take practice.

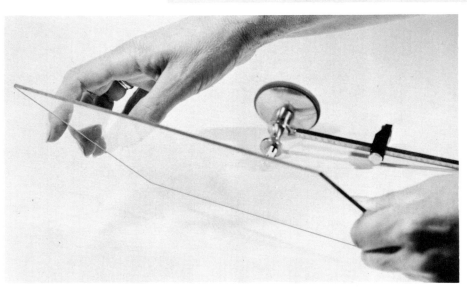

Illus. 9. When you have succeeded, turn the piece of glass upside-down.

Illus. 10. Tap with the side of the glass pliers along the scored line on the reverse side until the glass is cracked all round the circle.

Hold the device securely with your left hand in such a manner that your right hand, holding the cut, will reach over your left arm and as far as possible behind your left hand. This way, you can score the glass in a complete circle with a single movement of your right hand (or vice versa if you are left-handed), without interruption. This is important, because any interruption in the scored line makes it impossible to produce a perfect circle with smooth edges.

It is advisable to do your preliminary practicing on a cardboard support. When you have managed to score a circular line on a piece of glass, lay two pieces of corrugated cardboard on the table and place the glass plate upside-down upon it, that is, with the scored line underneath. With the side of the glass pliers, tap along the scored line until you see the glass crack, then turn the plate a little and continue tapping until the plate is cracked completely around the circle.

At this point, the circle is still held firmly in the glass square, so turn the glass over so

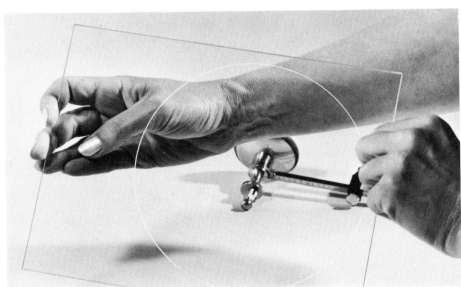

Illus. 11. Turn the glass over again so the scored side is up.

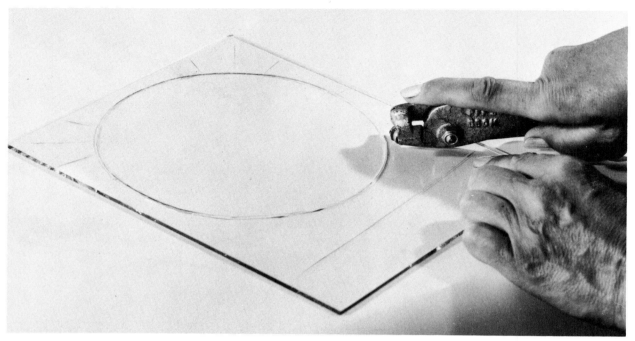

Illus. 12. On the "right" side of the glass, score radial lines outwards from the edge of the circle.

that the scored circle is up, and with the glass cutter, score radial lines outwards from the circumference starting about $\frac{1}{4}''$ to $\frac{3}{8}''$ from it. Carry the radial lines out to the edge of the square. It will be enough to score a diagonal line in each corner and another line to the right and another to the left of it. Now turn the glass over again and tap with the pliers on the diagonal lines. The glass will now crack and let go of the circle and your round, glass plate will lie perfectly whole before you.

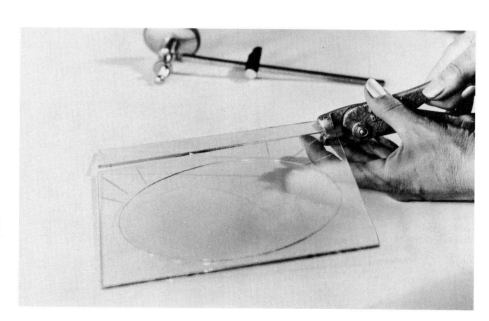

Illus. 13. Snap off any excess glass beyond the edges of the radial lines.

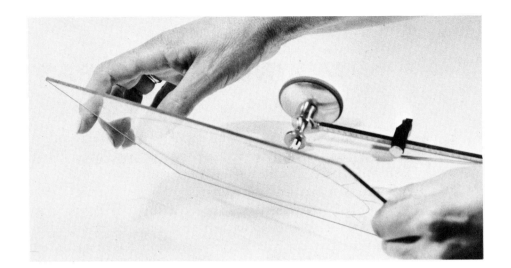

Illus. 14. Turn the glass over again, scored-side down.

Illus. 15. Tap with the side of the pliers along the radial lines, until . . .

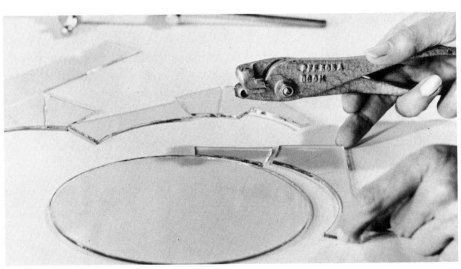

Illus. 16. . . . the glass circle is complete.

13

MIXING GLAS-O-PAST-X

Unlike most colors used in the glass and earthenware industry, Glas-O-Past-X colors are intermixable, which broadens the range of available colors enormously. In mixing, however, you must keep in mind a few important rules.

To begin with, you can mix all transparent Glas-O-Past-X colors directly on the surface that is to be colored. In doing this, squeeze a small quantity of paint from the two or three tubes involved and mix the colors on the glass before thinning with paint thinner or acetone. If you thin first and mix later, you will find it more difficult to obtain an even color. If this is not your intention, of course, it makes no difference.

Transparent red is an exception to the rule. Gold is used in the composition of this color; therefore, if you mix it with other colors, the other colors will predominate. Transparent red is redder at lower temperatures than at bending temperature. At bending temperature, depending on the composition of the glass, the color is a shade of red-purple.

When you shape a dish with this color, you will notice that the color develops a redder shade where it is enclosed between two pieces of glass than where you paint a single piece of glass on the upper surface. This is because the color is protected by a covering glass and receives slightly less heat.

However, when you paint a thick glass plate with transparent red Glas-O-Past-X, you can obtain other effects. To start, do not let the temperature rise higher than 1418° F. (770° C.)—cone 017, plus a few minutes extra firing to rise another 18° F. (10° C.). This means that you must file very thick glass as smooth and round as you possibly can. It is expecially worth the trouble, on occasions such as this, to have the glass edges polished before firing, for then nothing can go wrong. Thus, you have a ground glass plate on which you paint the transparent red color. Then lay the glass plate on a prepared forming dish and heat to 1418° F. (770° C.)—cone 017. You can use cone 016, and, using an automatic shut-off, lay the rod on the narrow part of the cone (Illus. 17). The result is a red-purple dish which looks deep blue when held against the light. A deep dish, set upon a white surface, shows this up clearly.

When mixed with white Glas-O-Past-X, transparent colors fire out to opalescent, pastel tints. These are very beautiful in combination with opaque colors.

The opaque colors of Glas-O-Past-X are also mutually intermixable, again with the exception of red. Nor is it possible to mix orange.

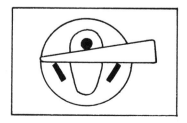

Illus. 17. When using an automatic shut-off, place the cone in this position.

Illus. 18. This handsome wall plaque was made by a nursery-school child using opaque Glas-O-Past-X paints.

The number of colors obtainable by mixing the opaque colors is practically countless. When opaque colors are mixed with white, the result is opaque pastel tints.

Opaque colors must not be mixed directly on the glass. Instead, use an odd piece of glass or an old dish for the mixing, and stir the colors thoroughly together.

A large piece of glass serves best for this, as it can also be used as a palette. Opaque Glas-O-Past-X colors have a totally different function from that of the transparent colors which you will be mainly using. With transparent paints, the colors can be set down side by side and a few lines in black or white painted on, but you cannot paint any kind of a design with them. You can, however, with opaque paints. These do not run, and even the finest lines remain visible after the firing. Red and orange will not lose their brilliance at bending temperature.

Opaque paints are at their loveliest when overlaid with a plate of undecorated glass. The color then achieves a look of depth. On the other hand, the color looks a little flat when opaque paints are fired on the open surface of glass.

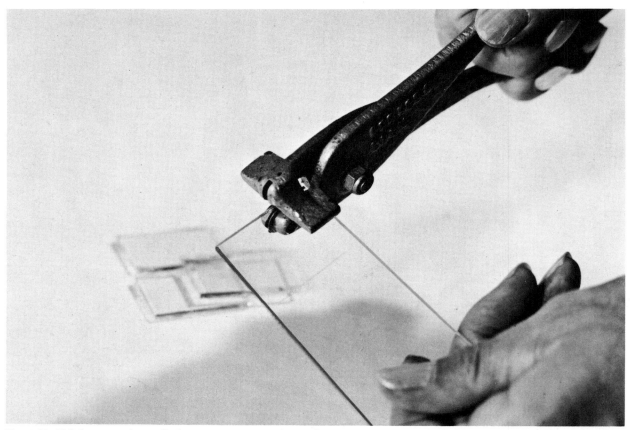

Illus. 19. With a number of glass squares such as these, you can make the lovely necklace in Illus. 20.

CONDUCT AN EXPERIMENT

The first thing to do is to become acquainted with your material and your best teacher will be some small pieces of glass. Don't plan any particular purpose for these pieces—just consider them as trial pieces only in order to test out the different materials and their possibilities.

Here are some of the things you need:

A number of tubes of Glas-O-Past-X in transparent and opaque colors.
A separation coating, or separator, for firing in the kiln.
A carborundum stone.
A can of denatured alcohol (shellac thinner).
A can of turpentine (paint thinner) or acetone.
A can of mica flakes.
A small roll of light-gauge, nickel-silver wire.
A small roll of heavy-gauge, nickel-silver wire.
A small roll of flat nickel-silver wire.

A #4 hog-bristle artist's paint brush, "bright" style (short bristles).
A quantity of clean rags.
A sieve.
Pieces of glass.
A pair of glass pliers (and a glass cutter if a separate one is needed).
A kiln.

To start, cut a few—let's say, six—strips of glass 2″ or 3″ long. These are called "blanks." File the edges nice and smooth with a carborundum stone (if you have a foot-power or motor-driven grindstone that runs at slow speed in water, all the better). You do not have to polish the edges. They will get slick and smooth enough in the heat of the kiln. Just get rid of the sharp edges.

When using the carborundum stone, always file away from yourself so that no splinters of glass will fly towards you. A face-shield or safety goggles are good to wear in any case. Both are inexpensive.

Wipe the glass thoroughly clean with a rag dipped in denatured alcohol (shellac thinner) and after that, hold it only by the edges with thumb and forefinger, so that your fingers do not touch the flat surfaces. Continue until you have six pieces of glass neatly laid out in a row. *It is necessary that any two pieces you heat together should be cut from the same kind of glass, so that they will expand and contract precisely the same in the kiln.* If they are not "compatible," fracturing can take place, even some time after they have cooled, although this is not likely to happen with small pieces.

Next, take a quantity of separator and mix it in a small dish. Add just enough water to cover, then stir for several minutes, mixing the material thoroughly. Pour the mixture through a fine sieve or an old, nylon stocking stretched over the mouth of a jar. The

Illus. 20. Plain window glass, colored with Glas-O-Past-X and fired in a kiln, produced this unique necklace.

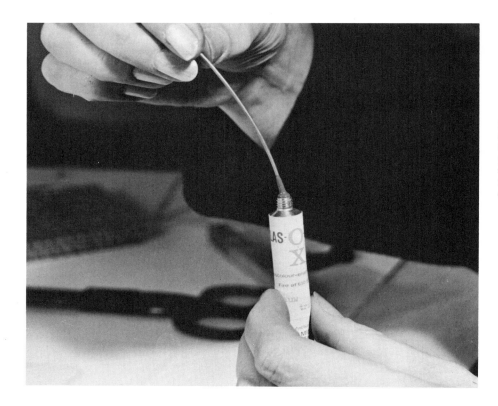

Illus. 21. When opening a new tube of Glas-O-Past-X, puncture the closing with a slim knitting needle and stir carefully.

material should have the same consistency as whipping cream before it is whipped, that is, quite fluid. If it is too thick, add more water while stirring, until it reaches the proper consistency. Press it through the sieve with a brush; then rinse the brush thoroughly under running water.

Squeeze the brush dry, dip it into the mixture, and paint the kiln shelf with a smooth, even coat of separator. It is important to leave as few ridges between strokes as possible, because every streak will be represented in the glass after the firing. Cover the kiln shelf so that not a single spot is left uncovered. This protects the shelf from the possibility of damage. The separating material will keep the glass from sticking to the shelf when it gets hot. If you don't use it, you will just provide the shelf with some unwanted decoration!

In winter, you can dry the shelf on a heater of some kind. In the summer, put it in the kiln and leave it there for a quarter of an hour with the power turned on to the lowest heat. Leave the kiln cover off during this operation.

When placed on a dry shelf, the glass object glistens brightly all over after cooling. If you lay the object directly on a damp shelf, however, the glass will take on a frosted look from the action of the moisture. This can be very attractive, but its appearance might puzzle you if you didn't know why it happened. If the kiln shelf is very wet when it is heated, it will break when the temperature rises.

Now back to our glass pieces. Open a tube of Glas-O-Past-X—a transparent, medium green, say. With a sharp object (ice-pick), prick a hole through the thin, lead film closing the opening. Take care not to squeeze the tube. As with oil paints in tubes, a little of the glass paste will protrude. Stick a knitting needle carefully through the bulge of paint, into the tube, and stir. Take care not to punch a hole through the tube! Stir the color this way every time you use it.

Now squeeze a small quantity of paint directly from the tube upon the glass. Spread it out evenly over the entire surface. If the Glas-O-Past-X is too thick to spread easily, you can thin the color with ordinary paint thinner. A lot of thinner makes a very light tint. The less thinner you use, the darker the tint will be.

Next, bend three horseshoe shapes from nickel-silver wire and lay two of them on the narrow edge of the painted glass and one on an unpainted piece of glass of the same size. Then scatter on one painted piece of glass a few flakes of mica. Lay the second piece of glass on a heater to dry.

After drying, lay the three pieces of glass on a kiln shelf, so they can't touch each other. Lay an unpainted piece of glass on the first one, and do the same with the now-dry second one. The third piece is covered with a piece of glass with the paint on top of it. You now have three double pieces of glass.

The result after firing (page 22): (a) The first piece shows a transparent color with silver spots (mica flakes) and color concentrations round the spots; (b) the second shows an enclosed cloudiness because the gases from the oily medium could not escape; (c) the third, with the color on top, is smooth and even.

Illus. 22. Three unusual wall plaques showing the individuality of their kindergarten creators.

Illus. 23. A large ceramic kiln is a wise investment because of its versatility. This economy model reaches a temperature of 2282° F. (1250° C.) and can be provided with an automatic shut-off, which is ideal for glass shaping.

THE KILN

Fundamentally, glass can be fired in any ceramic kiln. This does not hold true, however, of the enamelling kiln. A ceramic kiln and an enamelling kiln are based on two different principles. In a ceramic kiln, the temperature must be raised very slowly, and cooling must also take place at a relatively slow rate, which makes it most suitable for firing glass. In an enamelling kiln, the heat is brought up quickly, the piece is placed in the kiln while it is hot, and, as soon as it gets red-hot, is withdrawn. For this reason, all enamelling kilns must be provided with a hinged door on the front. Ceramic kilns, however, may be top-loaded or have a door that opens in front. *A ceramic kiln may not be opened while firing is going on.*

There is, of course, the combination kiln that can be used for glass bending, baking small pieces of earthenware, and, if it has a front-opening door, also for enamelling. Such a kiln can have a chamber as small as 10″ × 9″ × 10″ high, and sometimes even smaller. If the kiln is equipped with a rheostat-type, continuous switch, it is possible for you to control the temperature rise, bringing up the heat as quickly or as slowly as you please.

Also, the kiln has a peep-hole in the door, sometimes covered with Pyrex glass, so that you can watch what is going on in the kiln during the two or three hours of firing.

A kiln may be small enough to contain only one dish at a time, or perhaps a wall collage, or a number of costume jewelry pieces. When purchasing a kiln, try to get one in which no afterglow comes from the walls and ceiling after the heat is shut off. This could cause over-firing. So, choose a kiln equipped with lightweight refractory insulation bricks.

A large, ceramic kiln, however, is a necessity if you want to make large pieces or a number of pieces at the same time. Ceramic kilns are available in all sizes, up to and including the large, walk-in kind, but such a kiln is hardly for the hobbyist. The maximum size of a kiln having a rectangular chamber that can be used on ordinary 110-volt house current is about 12″ × 12″ × 13″ high, these measurements being made *inside* the firing chamber.

For a number of years, kilns have been available made in the shape of a hexagon or a heptagon. Such a kiln can measure as much as 15″ maximum diameter inside and 20″ high, and still be used on house current.

The most modern kilns are built of new materials developed especially for space exploration and the best are clad in stainless steel. These kilns require less current to accomplish a firing than a rectangular kiln of the same volume.

If you require a larger kiln than that mentioned above, you will have to have 220-volt current available for it. This is merely a matter of having an electrician bring a special wiring set-up from your fuse box to wherever you want the receptacle placed for the kiln to plug into. It is recommended that you study the kilns that are available to you locally and also send away for brochures from manufacturers of nationally known equipment. That way, you will not be sorry later that you rushed in and bought the first thing that showed up.

Any kiln you buy can be equipped with one of the several automatic shut-off devices available. This device works by means of a junior-size pyrometric cone. The cone is mounted

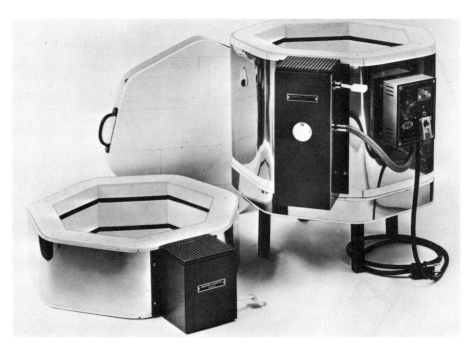

Illus. 24. This luxury model has heating coils in the removable top ring and is equipped with an automatic shut-off.

in the shut-off in such a way that, when it starts to bend at the proper shut-off temperature, the device takes over the movement and switches off the power. This makes kiln operation for glass shaping particularly easy.

Certain types of devices can be applied to any kiln drawing a maximum of 45 amperes of current. There are also devices that can be used on less current than this. If you get an automatic shut-off for your kiln, make sure that it is suitable for use with the maximum current your kiln uses.

For using an automatic shut-off, the kiln must be provided with a peep-hole on the front side, into which is inserted the tube that accepts the junior-size cone in operation. There is also available an automatic shut-off device that is equipped with a connected limit timer for extra safety. A kiln equipped with this device can be allowed to fire into the night without supervision. Discuss these matters with your ceramic supplies dealer for latest features and prices.

Do not buy a ceramic kiln for glass bending that is not equipped with an electric switch; that is, the kiln must not start up the moment you plug it in. In such a kiln, the temperature rises so fast that the glass cannot keep up with it and will crack. This can cause damage to the kiln. However, if you do decide that you want a certain kiln, only to find that it is not equipped with a switch, you can always have a switch installed. If you install a switch of the rheostat type—which provides a constantly increasing flow of current as the control knob is turned, a small increment at a time—you can then completely control the rate of temperature rise in the kiln.

Firing

Many people fear firing in a ceramic or glass-shaping kiln, as if it were a mountain to climb, yet these kilns are as easy to use as your kitchen oven, once you know how. Your first problem is loading the kiln.

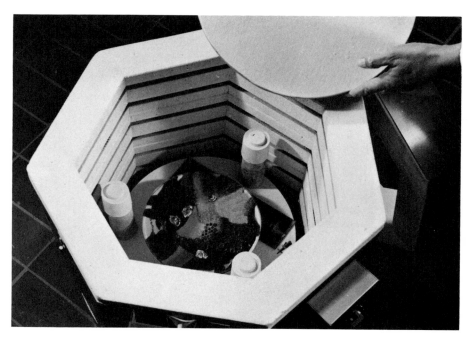

Illus. 25. A dish is placed on the first shelf. Notice the height of the shelf supports ready to receive the second shelf.

22

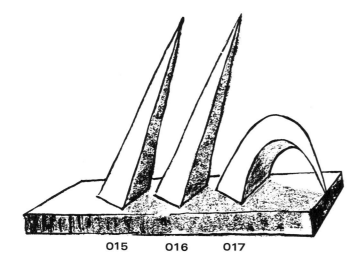

Illus. 26. You can get kiln cones for every temperature. Place three cones in a pat of clay with the one in the middle being the desired temperature. When the first cone begins to melt, watch carefully until the one in the middle bends. If the third cone bends you will know that you have over-fired.

015   016   017

Place three shelf supports in a multiple-sided kiln, or four in a rectangular firing chamber, and on these lay the kiln shelf with its separator-coated side up. If the kiln has heating elements in the floor, the shelf supports should be at least 4″ high. Otherwise, 1″ high is enough.

Lay the three doubled plates of glass you made (page 19) on the shelf after making sure that there is no paint on the edges of the pieces. Any contact between the paint and the separator coat must be avoided, because the paint will stick to the coating. To remove paint from the edges, use a rag dipped lightly in paint thinner.

Place a cone in the kiln, either sitting on the kiln shelf or on a shelf support of the right height to allow it to be seen through the peep-hole. You have a choice of using regular-size cones (2½″ high), or the junior size (1⅛″ high). Number 016 (called "cone oh-sixteen") should be about right. This cone bends at 1463° F. (795° C.) Whether you use a large or a small cone, the same number is indicative of the same bending temperature for each.

The proper way to place the cone is to take a small pat of clay and sit the wide end of the cone into it in such a position that the cone leans slightly to the right or to the left. This lean is necessary so that the cone will start to bend immediately upon reaching its bending temperature.

Cones are available for every desired temperature, each number indicating a different bending temperature. Ceramic craftsmen usually place three cones in a pat of clay. The cone in the middle indicates the desired temperature. The cone on the side towards which all three cones lean is the next-lower temperature cone, and on the other side, the next-higher. When the first cone bends, it is a warning to you that the middle cone will soon follow and for you to keep a sharp watch on the kiln. As soon as that cone begins to bend, shut the kiln off immediately. If you forget to watch the kiln and finally look in and see that the third cone is bending over, then you know beyond a doubt that you have over-fired the load.

If your kiln is equipped with an automatic shut-off switch, the tube projecting into the kiln through the peep-hole will accept a junior-size cone. If your kiln is equipped with a pyrometer (a meter calibrated in degrees for the direct reading of high temperatures) you do not need cones, as you can go by the temperature reading on the meter. However, for the first few firings, it is a good idea to use a cone along with the pyrometer to make sure that the meter reads correctly. If it does not read precisely the correct temperature when the cone bends, the temperature reading it gives is the one to be used when firing to that cone (the ceramist uses the word "cone" as synonymous with any of the precise firing temperatures). You should take the reading from the meter through several cone firings, and, if they vary even slightly, strike a mean between the highest and lowest readings and this will be the proper reading for that cone. This is called "calibrating" the meter.

The time taken by the kiln to reach the desired temperature also plays an important part in firing glass, as a cone will bend at other than its true bending temperature if the kiln is fired up too fast. For large pieces, cone 016, when fired at the proper rate of temperature rise, is correct. For firing small costume jewelry or decorative pieces, a slightly higher temperature is preferred—cone 015, 1481° F. (805° C.). These temperatures are suggested for firing the multi-sided kilns. If you are using a conventional kiln with a rectangular firing chamber, you would do better to fire at a somewhat lower temperature. The reason for this is that these kilns have very thick walls; therefore, there is considerable after-radiation once the kiln is shut off, which has the effect of prolonging the firing.

Before closing the kiln, check to make sure that none of the top plates has shifted its

Illus. 27. Another piece, a wall plaque, is placed on the second shelf. Because the corners project beyond the shelf, they are supported on separator-treated pieces of thin kiln-shelf material.

Three exciting examples of glasscrafting with Glas-O-Past-X: Above, a heavy glass bowl painted and formed in the kiln at a slightly too-high temperature which caused the interesting shape. At the left is a glass fish composed of "gems." (See page 61.) To make the stunning bowl candleholder at the right, see page 97.

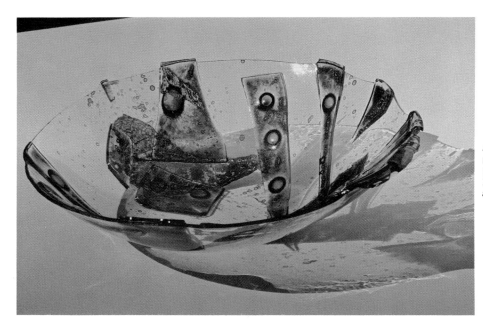

A dish made of a single piece of glass with pieces of Glas-O-Past-X-colored glass laid on and fired in a forming dish.

The dish at the upper left was made in the same way as the one in the photo at the top of the page. To achieve the bubble effect, see page 37. The large plate has glass grit enclosed in two pieces of glass, and the earrings are decorated with mosaic glass.

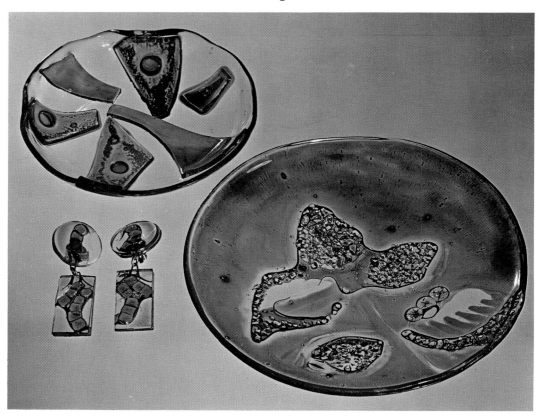

B

Pieces of broken glass were put together to form this stunning rooster. The fragments were painted with Glas-O-Past-X and sandwiched between two pieces of uncolored glass.

C

A blue plate with a delicate leaf motif made of enclosed glass grit. By Mevrouw Meyling-de Kat.

Glass and earthenware combine to make a striking plate. (See page 98.)

D

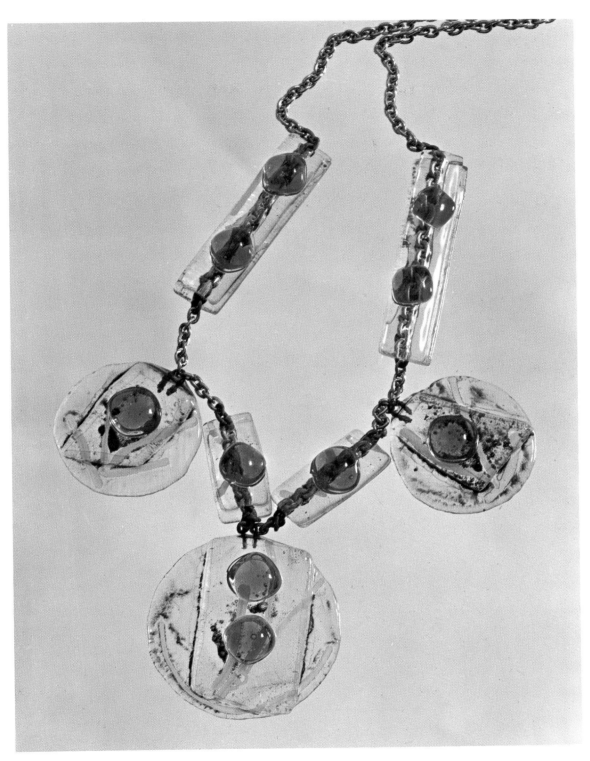

With very little effort, you can create a beautifully colored glass necklace such as this by either firing the chain between the pieces or slipping it through eyelets that you lay in between and fire with the glass.

There is no limit to the possibilities your glasscrafting with Glas-O-Past-X can produce. Ready-made findings are available for cuff links, rings, brooches, or any other glass jewelry you wish to mount.

F

Can you imagine hanging this lovely glass lamp shade over your dining room table? The slightest air movement will cause it to tinkle like an extravagantly expensive crystal chandelier!

G

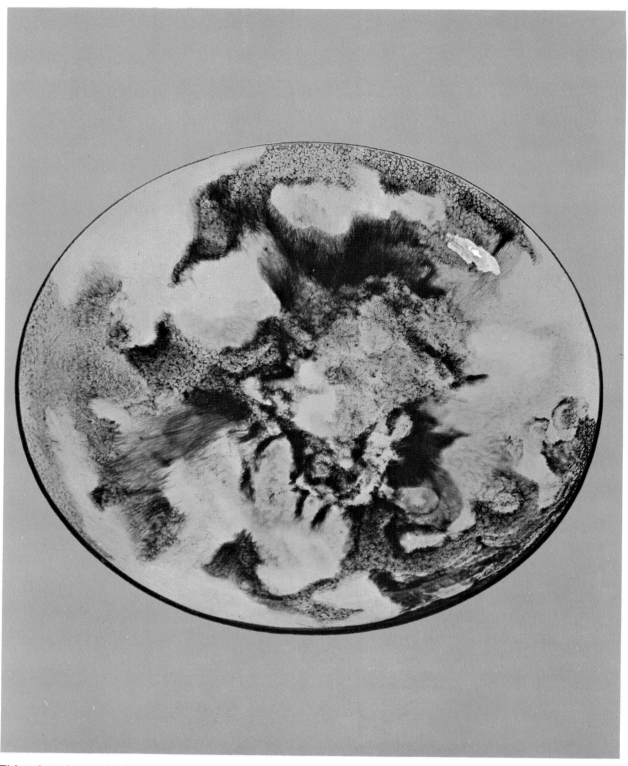

This plate is made from a single piece of glass painted with transparent blue and golden-yellow Glas-O-Past-X, with dark yellow surface stain sprinkled on. (See page 107.)

H

Illus. 28. The top rim has here been laid on the kiln in order to provide plenty of room above the glass piece.

position, and then close the door (either front or top) in such a way that it is propped open a crack. This allows for the escape of moisture from the kiln in the preliminary firing.

If your kiln has a rheostat-type, continuous switch, turn the kiln on to its lowest heating stage, then increase the current a little every twenty minutes. However, if your kiln is equipped with a standard, three-speed switch (Low, Medium and High), or with three tumbler switches in the same ranges, switch to a higher stage every half hour. This is exactly the same procedure followed in glaze-firing an earthenware object. After one hour, close the kiln.

A very small kiln for glass bending should only be turned up to stage 4 (if the switch is so marked) for glass firing, and never to "full on."

As soon as the cone shows the first sign of bending, shut the kiln off and after that you must not open the door until the entire device has become thoroughly cool. This does not mean cooled off to the warmth of your hand, but it must actually be cold. Depending on the size of kiln, this may take twenty-four hours or more. If you are in a hurry and open the kiln too soon, the glass will not yet be entirely relieved of its tension and will crack. It may not crack at once, either—perhaps not until several weeks have passed.

When the kiln is thoroughly cooled, open it and take out the glass. You now have three

hangers and, at the same time, a great deal of information that you can glean from the three different test pieces:

Illus. 30. Leave the kiln open a crack until a red glow appears shining from the kiln walls.

1. *Test with mica flakes.* In this, the color is evenly distributed with a concentration of color around the mica flakes. Such concentrations always appear whenever certain materials are buried in the paint. Moreover, there exist here and there light areas with a silvery edge. This happens particularly with large pieces.

2. *Test with the paint on the bottom glass plate.* This results in scum, which is caused by the gases generated when the vehicle carrying the pigment is burned out and which cannot escape. This feature has great decorative possibilities, which, unfortunately, are totally uncontrollable. Lovely colorations make an appearance.

3. *Test with the paint on the top plate.* Here the paint has melted out into a smooth, even layer.

When the glass has been fired to the correct temperature, the edges round off nicely and feel very smooth to the touch. The metal eyelet is melted firmly between the two layers of glass. In all three tests, the glass will seem to be colored throughout.

Checklist:

Cut the glass plates.
File the edges smooth with the carborundum stone, using long strokes away from yourself.
Clean the glass with denatured alcohol.
Shake a little separator into a bowl and pour on just enough water to cover.
Let soak for a few minutes.
Stir thoroughly with a brush.
Screen the material through a sieve (or nylon stocking) and thin as required.
Cover the kiln shelf with an even coat of separator.
Let dry thoroughly.
Open a tube of color and stir the contents with a knitting needle.
Squeeze a little bit of paint directly upon the glass.
Add a drop of paint thinner (or acetone, a quick drier).
Spread the paint out in an even coat.
Lay on a hanging eyelet and sprinkle a few mica flakes around on it.
Let dry thoroughly.
Lay a plate of uncolored glass on top.

Checklist of Kiln Practice:

When a kiln does not have heating elements in the floor, support the kiln shelf on 1"-high shelf supports.
When a kiln does have heating elements in the floor, support the kiln shelf on 4"-high shelf supports.
Place glass in the kiln and inspect carefully to see that nothing has shifted.
Place the cone inside, in front of the peep-hole or in the automatic shut-off.
Close the kiln, leaving the cover or door open a crack.
Switch the kiln on to Low.
With rheostat-type switch, increase power input every twenty minutes.
With the three-stage switch, step the power up every half hour. After one hour, close the kiln.
As soon as the cone starts to bend, shut off the kiln immediately.
Let the kiln and its contents become thoroughly cold before opening.

After each use, the separator should be cleaned off the kiln shelf, since it loses its resistant properties with firing. Usually, the layer flakes off by itself. If it does not, keep painting new layers over the old. After the next firings, the material will be on so thick that you can easily scrape it off with a putty knife.

Be sure to put the caps back on all tubes of paint to keep them from drying out. Should you forget this and the paint dries in the neck of the tube, put it aside and save it for when you are going to do a large piece. Then, snip the tube open directly under the neck and squeeze it empty; or, use a stiff brush. Rub the paint out on the glass, using a little thinner mixed with acetone. Glas-O-Past-X can be used to the last drop.

BENDING

GLASS

Illus. 31. Flat window glass was painted with Glas-O-Past-X, sprinkled with glass "grit," and bent into a dish shape in the kiln.

However incredible this may sound to many people, we actually do just this. We *do* bend glass. (Glass bending is also called slumping and sagging.)

Exactly what happens when you bend glass plates? First of all, glass weakens and turns soft when it is heated to a high temperature. Therefore, if you lay a round, glass plate on the rim of an earthenware dish and heat the assembly to the softening temperature of the glass, the glass will sag of it own weight and lie down on the inside of the earthenware supporting dish, thus taking on its shape. The kiln is then shut off. When cool, the glass becomes rigid, is no longer a flat plate, but has the shape of a dish.

Even though the process is a simple one, there are a few instructions you must keep in mind.

Your first need in glass shaping is for two glass blanks having the same diameter as the rim of the earthenware forming dish. They can be a little smaller, but not even *a bit* larger.

For your first test, use broken show-window glass—this is thicker than ordinary window glass. Your glass dealer will probably have a number of odd pieces on hand for you to select from. Have him cut the glass for you in two circles of the right size. It will not hurt if the glass has a few scratches on it, so long as they are not too deep. Broken show-window glass is recommended for your experimenting as it is so much less expensive than new glass.

Unglazed, earthenware bowls to use for forms are available at all craft houses. Later, of course, you will be able to make your own forming dishes in your own kiln. (See page 35.)

Since round, glass plates are always cut from square plates of glass, each cutting always creates waste pieces of the corners. When the glass dealer cuts the circles for you, tell him you want these waste pieces, too, as you will be able to make good use of them. At the same time, ask him for any other pieces of uncolored, waste glass he is willing to part with. You can make especially good use of glass strips. It is seldom the glass dealer will charge anything for this material—and don't forget, frosted glass and textured glass will serve your purposes equally well.

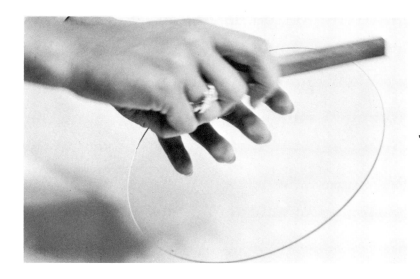

Illus. 32. When filing glass edges with the carborundum stone, always file away from yourself. An added precaution is wearing safety goggles or a face-shield.

Now that you have an unglazed bowl and suitable glass circles, you are ready to get started. File the edges of the glass with a carborundum stone, taking care to file with long strokes and to *file away from yourself only*. If you file towards yourself, or scrape back and forth with the carborundum stone, you may get a shower of fine, glass splinters in your face. Avoid this, even if you are wearing safety goggles or a plastic face-shield, which is a good idea in any case. If the edge is not smooth before firing, it will not be smooth after firing, either.

Take care in filing that you make the edges rounded enough so that they will not cut through the separator coating you will put on the forming dish later. After filing, clean the glass thoroughly with a rag dipped in denatured alcohol (shellac thinner), and then wipe it dry with a soft, flannel rag. The cleaner and brighter the glass, the better the result will be.

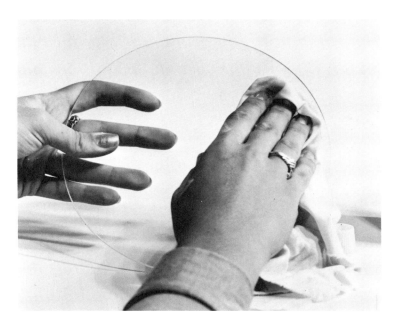

Illus. 33. After filing, always clean the glass with denatured alcohol. If the glass is immaculate to start with, the finished product will be brighter.

29

Illus. 34. Painting the glass with Glas-O-Past-X. Always paint with broad strokes. Delicate little lines will be lost in the finished product.

Illus. 35. If you want, you can sprinkle on mica flakes to add texture.

Illus. 36. Here, large pieces of broken glass are placed on the plate with a tweezers.

Next, open a tube of transparent, golden-yellow Glas-O-Past-X and stir the color evenly throughout with a knitting needle. Squeeze between 1″ and 2″ of paint into the middle of one glass plate. Add a few drops of paint thinner. A glass eye-dropper is the best thing to use for this. Mix the paint and thinner together; then draw with the brush a number of curved lines from the middle of the glass out to the edge. Try to do this as loosely and quickly as possible, for this is not intended to be a fussy kind of decoration. Use a broad, flat, hog-bristle brush, called a "bright."

Next, open a tube of black Glas-O-Past-X, stir up the contents, and squeeze a small quantity out alongside the middle of the glass plate. Add a few drops of paint thinner, but do not stir. With a wad of paint under the brush, draw black, curved lines alongside of and on top of the previous lines made with yellow paint. Because the paint thinner is lying on the glass plate and you scoot the paint through it, the two get only slightly mixed together, which is precisely what you want. Take care, however, that not the least trace of paint gets on the edge or underside of the glass. If any does get there, remove it with a little acetone on a rag. Now lay the work aside to dry a little.

The coating material should be thinner for preparing the forming dish than for painting the kiln shelf. If you are accustomed to glazing earthenware, you may go ahead and apply separator to the inside of the dish the same way you would apply glaze.

If you are not familiar with this procedure, however, do this: Fill the dish about two-thirds full of separator. Pour the material quickly out of the dish, back into its original container, at the same time turning the dish in your hands so that the material covers the entire inside surface evenly. Because of the porous nature of unglazed clay, the separator will sink in and deposit a thin layer against the surface. The longer the mass of material is left in the dish, the thicker the coating becomes, making the bowl very wet.

However, do not leave it too long as this will not only waste the material but will also

Illus. 37. Pour thin separator into the forming dish, filling the dish about two-thirds full.

Illus. 38. Then, pour the separator back into the pitcher, at the same time turning the dish around so that the separator reaches the entire inside of the dish.

Illus. 39. Lay the plate carefully on the forming dish.

Illus. 40. Feel all round the edges to make sure that the glass does not protrude beyond the rim of the forming dish.

Illus. 41. Then lay the second, unpainted, piece of glass on top and feel round the edges again.

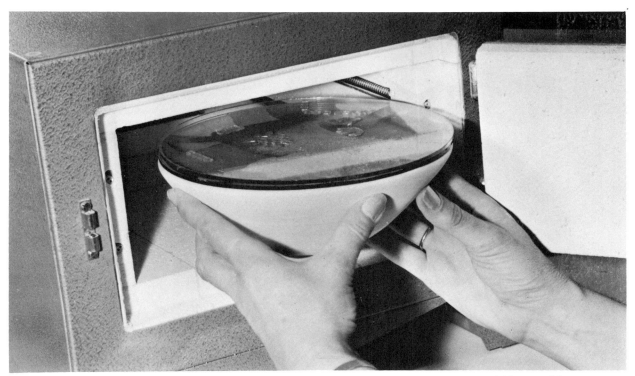

Illus. 42. When placing your work in the kiln, take care you do not shift anything.

cause streaks in it and these streaks will set off on the glass during the shaping process. Therefore, you must learn to pour the material out skilfully and quickly. Practice a few times with a *glazed* dish, so that you can use all the material over again without waste. When you feel that you have the knack of it, you can go ahead and coat the clay forming dish. (Naturally, you never use a glazed dish for firing.) Let the coating dry thoroughly.

When you lay the glass plate on the rim of the dish, make absolutely sure that the glass does not project out over the rim of the dish on one side and fall inside the rim on the opposite side. This would cause the glass to crack and spoil all your work. See to it, also, that you do not damage the separator in placing the plate, as any unevenness in the coating interferes with the sagging of the glass.

If you are using a glass smaller in diameter than the forming dish, take extreme care in placing it in the dish that you do not scrape the coating with your fingernails. That, too, will interfere with proper shaping in the kiln.

Then place the unpainted glass circle on top.

This may all sound rather complicated, but actually, the procedure is so simple that it practically goes by itself.

Fire the piece as directed on page 22. The remarkable thing about glasswork is that the glass always goes into the kiln looking plain and comes out shining with beauty.

It goes without saying that, when you use a forming dish as described above, you do not have to coat the kiln shelf with separator. Only when you fire flat pieces do you need to protect the kiln shelf in this manner.

You can put several pieces into the kiln at the same time. In doing so, however, maintain a separation of 3″ to 4″ between the glass and the kiln shelf (or kiln cover) above it. The reason for this is that kiln shelves absorb the heat of firing. Then, when the kiln is shut off,

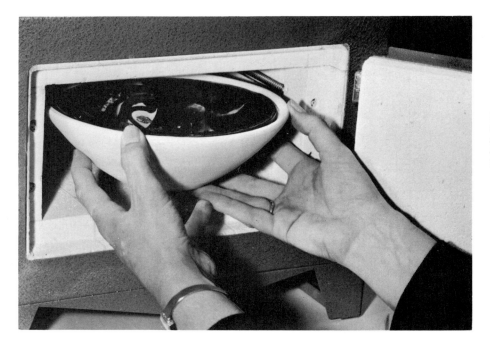

Illus. 43. After making sure the kiln is absolutely cooled off, open the door, and there is your finished dish.

they radiate this absorbed heat back into the kiln chamber. This extra radiation may have the effect of over-firing the glass beyond its actual softening temperature. The effect is not great on flat pieces, but it must be avoided in glass-shaping work. Let the glass dishes and the kiln cool off thoroughly before opening to prevent cracking the work.

The following signs indicate that the work has been over-heated: The bottom of the dish bulges upwards, sometimes as high as the rim of the dish. In even more serious cases of over-heating, the glass melts and flows down into the bottom of the forming dish, leaving sharp points standing up around the edges. This may have a discouraging ring to it, but remember that none of it has to happen. If it does happen, all is not lost. Save every piece of over-heated or cracked glass. You can make fine wall plaques out of these pieces, because they are a very special kind of glass that you cannot pick up anywhere. You can over-heat some glass on purpose just to provide yourself with some of this handsome material for special projects.

Checklist for Shaping Glass Dishes:
Cut two round, glass plates the same diameter as the forming dish.
File the edges smooth and rounded, *filing with long strokes away from yourself.*
Clean the glass thoroughly with denatured alcohol.
Open the tube and stir the paint.
Thin the paint directly on one glass plate with paint thinner.
Draw curved lines in a star shape out to the edges, but do not cover the plate entirely with paint.
Open a tube of black Glas-O-Past-X and stir it up.
Use the thinned paint to draw the same kinds of lines as before across the glass, letting the paint run over and beside the preceding lines, but only on part of the plate.
Let the paint partially dry.
Thin separator and fill the forming dish two-thirds full.
Pour it out skilfully and quickly, turning the dish in your hands as you do so.
Let it dry thoroughly; then lay the painted glass plate exactly on the forming dish.
Lay the second plate on top. Place it in the kiln, taking care that the glass does not shift.
Heat the kiln slowly to 1463° F. (770°–795° C.)— exactly cone 016.
Let the kiln get thoroughly cold before unloading.

34

MAKING A FORMING DISH

A forming dish is a dish of baked clay, which is unglazed and which serves as a negative form for the glass. You can buy such a forming dish ready-made, but it will have more of a personal touch if you design the dish yourself. You can do this, because you own a kiln. In forming the dish, work carefully so that you will have a good-looking, well-worked piece. This will naturally take some time, but you can use the forming dish for a long, long time. When you are through with it and replace it with another, you can coat it with glaze and fire it.

Use lightly grogged clay for making the forming dish. (Grog is ground-up firebrick that is added to clay to keep sculptured objects of earthenware from exploding in the kiln.) Use only the *finest* grog to give the inner surface of the dish a smooth, even texture. (The glass will hang up on coarse grog.)

Here is how to do it: Choose a dish or a bowl that is not too deep from the household supply. It can be made of glazed earthenware, metal or glass. Protect the tabletop with a sheet of plastic and lay the bowl upside-down upon it. Cover the outside with a layer of water-soaked facial tissues so that not even the tiniest spot remains uncovered.

Keeping on the sheet of plastic on the table, roll out a lump of clay to a thin sheet, the same way you would roll out biscuit dough. Use a rolling pin bought especially for the purpose, though. (Do not use your kitchen rolling pin or you may be picking half-baked bits of clay from between your teeth the next time you serve biscuits.)

Set the dish right-side up in the middle of the rolled-out sheet of clay; then take the plastic sheet by its four corners and bring them together, stretching the plastic as tightly as possible round the dish. Turn the dish over, remove the plastic sheet, and press the clay down firmly against the form, that is, the dish. Trim the excess clay away from the rim and

Illus. 44. When rolling out the clay, use a special rolling pin bought for just that purpose.

Photograph by J. M. Anderson. From "Ceramic Creations" by Robert Fournier.

let the clay get somewhat hard. This must not take too long, because clay shrinks upon drying and would start to pinch the bowl. This would be followed by cracking. As soon as the clay has stiffened a little, therefore, carefully remove the dish and place into it the clay bowl formed on its outside. This will provide a support for the clay while you work on it. The rim of clay now projects above the rim of the bowl and this you must now work over into a smooth, rounded edge. After that, let the clay stiffen further.

After the clay becomes stiff enough that it can stand to be removed from the support of the dish, smooth out any seams that may have formed on the inside from the overlapping of the tissues, and then let the clay dry thoroughly

The time needed for drying varies a great deal. In winter, with the heat on in a house, it will take about 10 to 14 days, depending upon the thickness of the clay. If you live in a part of the country where the summers are moist and cool, it could at that time of year take three or four weeks. Clay must always be dried in a dark, cool, and above all, breeze-free place. If you do not follow these rules, the dish will inevitably be deformed.

When the form is good and dry, sand the inner surface smooth with a medium-grit garnet paper. Fire the dish in the kiln at a temperature of 1481°–1580° F. (805°–860° C.)—cone 015–013. This temperature is lower than that at which earthenware is ordinarily fired. It is done this way to keep the forming dish quite porous so that the air trapped under the glass can escape as it expands with the heat; otherwise, even without over-heating, you would find the bottom bulged upwards. Therefore, it is safer when making a home-made forming dish to prick a tiny hole in it somewhere, through which the super-heated air can escape, the same as you would prick a hole through an eggshell.

Do this before the clay becomes completely hard, and use a knitting needle. If you want to design the shape of your own forming dish, start out as described above, using only a thin layer of clay wrapped around the dish. When the clay is removed from the form after stiffening, you have a good foundation to work with in forming a more personal design by shaping the clay as you desire. However, first let the basic form get leather-hard so that it will not fall out of shape while you are working on it.

Be extremely careful that you do not make the wall of your home-made forming dish too thick. The forming dish also soaks up heat and, when the wall is too thick, gives off too much radiation after the kiln has been shut down.

Checklist for Making Forming Dishes:

Choose a dish or bowl that is not too deep.
Turn it upside-down on the table.
Cover the outside of the dish with wet facial tissues.
Lay a large sheet of plastic on the table.
Roll out a lump of clay mixed with fine grog to a thin sheet.
Set the dish right-side up in the middle of the clay sheet.
Grasp the underlying plastic by the four corners and pull the plastic as tightly as possible around the dish.
Turn the dish over again and press the clay down tightly on the form.
Remove the excess clay around the rim.
Let the clay stiffen; then take away the form.

Now set the clay dish inside the form.
Let the clay get leather-hard; rub all seams down smooth, and prick a small hole somewhere through the dish.
Work over the sharply cut-off rim until it is smoothly rounded.
Take the clay dish out of the form.
Let the clay dry thoroughly in a cool, dark and breeze-free place.
From time to time, hold the clay form against your cheek as a test. If the clay feels cold, it is still damp. Dry clay is at room temperature and feels neither warm nor cold when held against your cheek.
Sand the dish smooth on the inside with medium-grit garnet paper.
Fire the clay, bringing the temperature up slowly to 1481°–1580° F. (805°–860° C.)—cones 015–013.

A DISH DECORATED WITH PIECES OF BROKEN GLASS

For this project, cut a round disc from double-strength window glass. A broken pane will yield sufficient material inexpensively. Keep the left-over pieces of waste glass and use these for the dish you are going to make. File the edges of the glass circle until they are smooth and round. At the risk of being repetitious: File *away* from yourself! Don't think you can skip the filing because the heat of firing rounds off the edges. This may be true, but the sharp, raw edge of the circle can cut through the layer of separator in such a way that you will not be aware of it, since such penetration involves only very tiny areas. The result is, of course, that the glass "hangs up" on that one tiny place (or several) while the rest of the dish sags into place as it should. This results in an unattractive dish.

Clean the glass plate thoroughly with denatured alcohol. This is particularly necessary when you are using a broken window-pane, because remains of putty are often present on

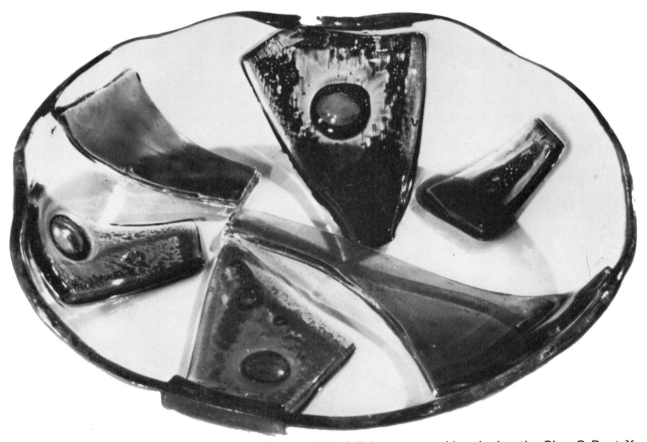

Illus. 45. The decorative air bubbles in this completed dish are caused by placing the Glas-O-Past-X-painted fragments paint-side down. The smoothly colored pieces were placed paint-side up. Another deliberate accident—the slight deformation of the dish—was caused by over-heating the kiln.

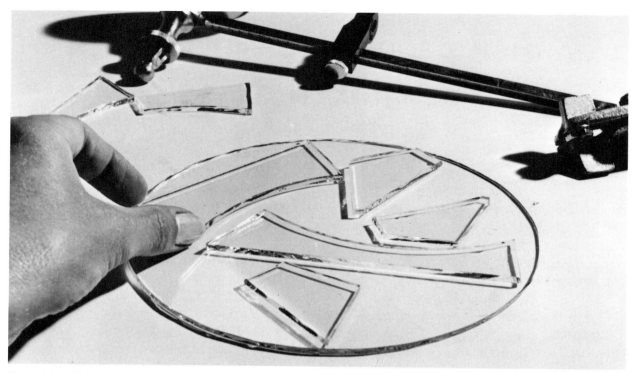

Illus. 46. After a circle of glass was cut out, the leftover fragments were placed on the circle.

the glass. First, scrape the dirt away with a knife, and then wash with alcohol, making sure that you get the glass clean enough to be able to see your face reflected in it. Then file the edges of the remaining pieces of glass.

You do not have to be as thorough in filing these as with the glass circle. It is enough just to remove the sharp edges.

Lay the glass fragments in a random pattern on the glass plate. Then arrange them in a

Illus. 47. The pieces of glass were colored with transparent blue Glas-O-Past-X.

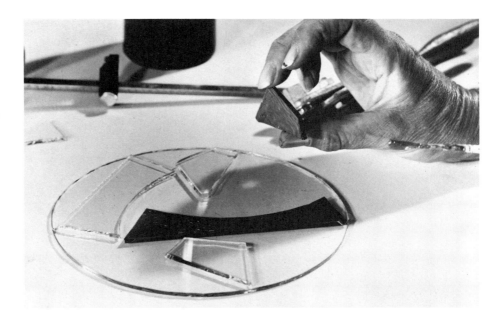

Illus. 48. Some of the pieces are laid paint-side down on the glass.

pleasing design, and pick them up one by one and color them. (Do not color the large, circular glass plate.) Lay some of the pieces with the painted-side down; others with the painted side up. Where the pieces are laid painted-side down, air bubbles will form between the plates of glass, while those pieces laid with the painted-side up will show an even layer of color. (See color page B.)

Illus. 49. Here, the glass pieces are all in place and painted.

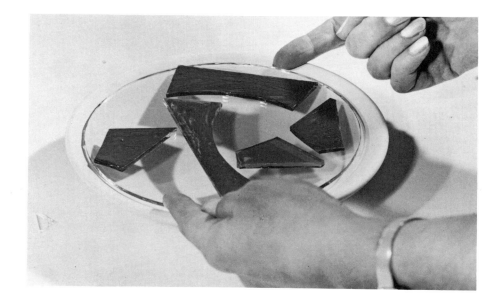

Illus. 50. The glass assembly is carefully set on a separator-coated forming dish.

Next, lay the glass assemblage on a forming dish coated with separator. Heat the kiln to 1463° F. (795° C.)—or cone 016; then let it cool down thoroughly. Long, slow cooling prevents cracking the dish. The dish in Illus. 45 was slightly over-heated and, for that reason, the glass began to sag to one side—a case of a "deliberate" accident, and it came out looking fine. This practice is not recommended, of course, until you have gained complete mastery of your techniques and materials.

Illus. 51. Then, it is placed in the kiln. When using separator-coated forming dishes, there is no need to coat the kiln shelf.

A SMALL

WALL PLAQUE

Illus. 52.

Take two glass plates measuring about 8″ × 10″. If your kiln is too small to accept so large a workpiece, adapt the size to fit, as it is impossible to fire a glass plate that is larger than the kiln shelf because such a plate would overhang the shelf and, when the latter shrank upon cooling, it would pull the glass pieces apart.

File the edges as usual with a carborundum stone. Just file away the sharp edges; then clean the glass thoroughly. Afterwards, paint one (or more) kiln shelf with separator. Let the coating get good and dry.

It is a good practice to have shelves and forming dishes already coated with a separator as it saves unnecessary waiting for the coating to dry. In case you forget whether you did this or not, you cannot tell by simply looking at a shelf whether it has a fresh layer on it or if it has been fired (and therefore unusable). The old layer does not always chip off after firing. So, a simple check is to rub your finger over the shelf. If a fine powder rubs off, the coating is fresh. A fired layer will not turn your finger white. If you make up shelves and forms in advance, you must take special care that the separator is smooth on the edges. If any roughness shows, touch up the spots where it has crumbled away, using a fine brush dipped in thinned separator.

Choose a tube of any transparent color of Glas-O-Past-X. Paint a few lines on the glass with a wide brush and rinse the brush in paint thinner. Choose a second transparent color and paint lines in the spaces between the first lines, but do not cover the entire glass with paint. Leave enough room for further division of the surface. Now, take a raw potato and cut it crosswise through the middle and make a stamp of simple design.

If you do not know what a potato stamp is, this is what you do: Scratch a diamond shape

Illus. 53. A delightfully designed and colored plaque made by a nursery-school child.

into the cut end of the potato; then carve away the rest of the potato outside the diamond shape. You will then have a diamond-shaped stamp. You can make any kind of simple design this way, either geometrical or figurative. Birds and fish are especially easy to do. After carving, dry off the cut surface of the potato with a rag or paper towel and brush the surface with a layer of unthinned, black Glas-O-Past-X. Then press the potato stamp down on the glass surface, just as you would a rubber stamp. Repeat the impression a couple of times, repainting the stamp with a fresh layer of paint before each impression.

You can stamp directly on the bare glass, or on transparent paint.

For inclusions, use very small pieces of thin sheet copper, or use some copper washers— these are used with copper rivets in certain kinds of leather work. Lay the washers on the glass, then scatter fine mica flakes on the paint. Finally, bend two hanger-eyes from heavy-gauge nickel-silver wire and lay these on the glass in a snakelike strip equidistant from the corners; then cover the assembly with the second, clean sheet of glass.

The paint does not have to dry, for the inclusions prevent the two glass plates from touching each other and squeezing out the paint. During the beginning of the firing there is time enough for the Glas-O-Past-X to dry.

When putting the top on the kiln (or closing the kiln door), make sure you leave it open a crack to provide escape for the gases given off by the drying paint. Take care, too, that there is no trace of paint on the edges of the glass. If you see any, wipe it away immediately.

Lay the two (or more) plates in the kiln and heat to the softening point of the glass. Take

Illus. 54. Another child's plaque which includes pieces of mosaic glass.

care that at least one piece of glass is visible through the peep-hole so that you can watch what goes on in the kiln. When you can watch the process, you can keep everything under control; therefore, never block the peep-hole with a kiln shelf, shelf support, or anything else by placing it too close to the hole.

If you are using a pyrometric cone, use an alarm clock or a bell-ringing timer to remind you to look into the kiln at definite intervals. This will prevent disappointment, for glass that is over-heated starts to melt too soon.

Still, a little over-heating can create an interesting effect. Glass starts to bulge just before it is over-heated too much. Right then is the time to shut off the kiln and the bulge will stay just as it is. Glass fired directly on the kiln shelf can absorb more heat than glass sagging in a form. That "more" means 18°–36° F. (10°–20° C.). more.

If you lay several glass plates, or glass plates and dishes, on shelves at different heights in the kiln, always put the dish on the *top* shelf in a kiln that has heating elements in the floor. If the kiln does not have floor elements, set the dish on the bottom shelf. That is the place where the kiln is just a few degrees cooler than the rest of the firing chamber. If you fire dishes and flat, glass plates alternately, that is, each kind in separate firing, use cone 015 for the flat glass plates.

Do not forget that the separation between the glass and the shelf or ceiling surface above the dish must be at least 4″. This applies only to a glass plate lying on a forming dish.

When flat glass plates are being fired, the temperature in the kiln must be raised somewhat

43

more slowly. Kiln shelves will stand quick temperature changes better than earthenware, but they pass heat more slowly. *If the kiln temperature is allowed to rise too quickly, the glass will heat up sooner than the kiln shelf, and this can lead to cracking.* This type of crack can be distinguished from a crack caused by cooling too fast, because the edges formed by the crack are melted and rounded off. A crack formed when the glass is cold has sharp edges. Keep it in mind, then, that the *thinner* the kiln shelf you use, the less trouble you are likely to have from cracking because of too swift a temperature rise.

Always let fired wall plaques cool off for a very long time—up to 48 hours. Opening the peep-hole, door, kiln cover, or any other opening in the kiln is to be strictly avoided during the cooling-off process.

Checklist for Making a Wall Plaque:

Cut two plates about 8″ × 10″ in size.
File the sharp edges from the plate with a carborundum stone.
Clean the glass with denatured alcohol (shellac thinner).
Choose a transparent color (red) of Glas-O-Past-X.
Draw a few wavy lines on the glass with a flat brush.
Rinse the brush in paint thinner.
Choose a second and a third transparent color (say, blue and green).
Draw a few wavy lines on the glass with these colors.
Rinse the brush in paint thinner.

44

Cut a potato crosswise through the middle and make a stamp of it.

Dry off the cut surface and brush it with unthinned, black paint.

Press the stamp against the glass.

Brush some more paint on the stamp, print it off, and so on.

Rinse brush in paint thinner.

Lay some copper washers on the glass.

Strew fine mica flakes over the paint in a snakelike strip.

Bend two hanger-eyes from heavy-gauge nickel-silver wire and lay them on the glass.

Lay the second, blank glass plate on the decorated plate.

Place the glass plates on the kiln shelf in the kiln.

Bring the kiln temperature up very slowly. Heat the kiln to about 1481° F. (about 805° C.)—cone 015.

During the final 90° F. (54° C.) rise, watch the kiln through the peep-hole.

Shut down the kiln when the edges of the glass round off from the heat; or, wait a little longer, until the glass has started to bulge a little.

Let the closed kiln cool off slowly, preferably for 48 hours.

Illus. 56. The rooster is composed of colored glass fragments enclosed between two glass plates. By Mevrouw Meyling-de Kat. (See front cover for color effect.)

A GLASS WALL COLLAGE

To make a glass collage, gather together all the pieces of glass you can find, concentrating on thick pieces. Take the bottoms and the necks of glasses, a broken glass figurine, beads, salve jars, carafes, thick face-cream jars. The quantity of glass you can get together is surprising, especially when you get friends and acquaintances into the act.

For a base, use a sheet of wire-reinforced glass. This glass has the advantage of being supported by its metal grid when the strain resulting from the different kinds of glass becomes too great. This does not mean that cracks will not occur in the glass, but only that they will not be serious. Even though a piece might fall out, the structure of the wire-glass ensures that no single crack will destroy your work. Wire-glass has two sides. One side is completely smooth, while on the other side, the surface dips in a little at each crossing of the supporting wires. If the glass is colored on the side that is slightly textured, then the paint, which is rather fluid, collects in the surface dips. Because these are equally distributed over the glass, you will get a colorful lattice-work under the glass which you will lay on top.

Remember, for the glass to stick well with a minimum of strain, you must be sure to coat the under-plate with Glas-O-Past-X, unless you use glas-dust which you have colored yourself (see page 107).

Never set a glass jar, however thick it might be, mouth down against the under-plate. The air in it expands, cannot get out, and thus inflates the jar. In most cases, the jar will not crack, but a thin, and therefore weak, spot will occur in the wall collage. However, if you place it with the mouth of the jar up, it will collapse in an unpredictable manner (see color page N).

At the softening point, bottle necks tend to bend towards one side—*which* side should depend on *you*. When the bottle neck is cut off square, you must tilt the kiln shelf down slightly in the direction you want the neck to fold. If the neck is cut off at an angle, it will automatically bend over towards the lowest side. Never place bottle bottoms on the kiln shelf in such a manner that air is trapped under the kick.

It is not always necessary to color the glass that is laid on the bottom plate. The remarkable fact is that, in consequence of the light diffraction of the randomly shaped glass, combined with the intensely brilliant colors of the paint, the uncolored glass, after softening, *looks* as if it were colored through and through. Place here and there, among the transparent colors, a small accent of a vivid color of opaque Glas-O-Past-X. Cover these colors with uncolored glass. In this way, you achieve great depth of color.

Heat to about 1454° F. (790° C.)—cone 016. In addition to glass, melt into the collage anything that does not burn—coarse and fine copper screen, nails and screws and all kinds of metal objects, with one exception—brass. Brass is an alloy of copper and zinc. Because zinc has a repelling action on glass, brass has the same effect, with the result that the glass will not stick together. You can include iron, however. Iron crumbles after heating, but, because it is enclosed by glass, that presents no problem. Also try shaping figures of flattened, nickel-silver wire. The $\frac{1}{8}$″ (approximately) wire can be easily bent and you can let it stand up enough that the glass will fold round it. Also consider using copper tubing—in brief, put your imagination to work and make a wall collage that is your very own creation. (See color pages I and M.)

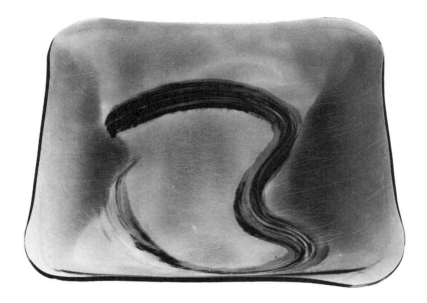

Illus. 57. An optical illusion of depth was created on this square dish colored with transparent smoky topaz Glas-O-Past-X, over which a broad brush loaded with black was dragged. The crackle effect is the result of taking the plate out of the kiln before it was completely cooled.

Illus. 58. This dish is decorated with transparent green Glas-O-Past-X with liquid gold brushed on. By Monica van Vlijmen.

Illus. 59. Here, two square pieces of ribbed glass were painted and set crosswise on each other in a round forming dish.

Illus. 60.

SANDWICHED GLASS

Making dishes out of two plates of glass gives you an endless number of possibilities above and beyond what you can do with only one plate. (Use double-strength glass, and cut one circle 1/10″ smaller in diameter. File the edges smooth and round with a carborundum stone, and clean the glass with alcohol.) For example, snip random designs out of copper screening. Clean the screen with alcohol and lay it in a solution of sodium bisulphate (sold commercially as Sparex), which is a pickling compound available at all craft supply shops. Pick it up with tweezers, wash under running water. Dry the screen with a clean cloth, and lay it on one plate covered with Glas-O-Past-X in smoky-topaz. This is a transparent color. Next, brush a thin coat of transparent yellow Glas-O-Past-X over the copper screen. Scatter a few pieces of colorless, transparent glass mosaic here and there, and lay the plate on the separator-coated forming dish. Carefully lay the second, clean plate on the decorated one and let them, in the heat of the kiln, sag together into the form.

After cooling, the copper screen appears to have become much redder, while a concentration of color has taken place around the uncolored, glass mosaic pieces. Because the glass round the edges sagged inwards and that over the mosaic pieces could not, the air caught between the plates could not escape. This causes large areas filled with air to become enclosed, giving the glass an individual character. Whenever you enclose fireproof materials between two pieces of glass, it is not necessary to let the paint dry before firing. The space which these materials create between the two glass plates is so great that all the gases resulting from the firing can get out.

Do not use a deep forming bowl for a dish that is to be made up of two plates of glass unless you make the upper plate about 1/10″ smaller in diameter. Two plates of the same size in a deep bowl will not produce a good-looking edge, because one plate sticks out over the other one. For this reason, the edges do not unite in a perfect match, and you can always see, by looking at the edges, that two glass plates were used.

Very deep forming dishes cannot be used. The glass stretches too much and therefore comes under more strain than it is able to stand.

Do not lay the glass askew on the forming dish, or it will turn into an asymmetrical dish. Especially, do not set the forming dish to one side in the kiln and thus too close to the heating elements. This will cause the glass to sag unequally. Of course, this does not apply to flat pieces.

The glass will always be most beautifully and regularly shaped when the forming dish is set exactly in the middle of the kiln shelf. This carries no disadvantage with it, for you can at the same time lay a large number of smaller flat pieces on the shelf around it. In this case, do not forget to treat the kiln shelf with a coat of separator.

Checklist for Making a Dish of Sandwiched Glass:

Cut two circular plates out of double-strength glass, both the circles the same diameter for a flat dish; but for a deep dish, cut the top circle 1/10″ smaller in diameter.
Using a carborundum stone, file the edges with long strokes until they become smooth and rounded.
Clean the glass thoroughly with denatured alcohol.
Snip figures out of fairly coarse copper screen.
Pull the screen into shape and ravel it out where necessary.
Clean the screen with alcohol and lay it in a solution of sodium bisulphate.
Cover the entire glass plate with a thick layer of transparent, smoky-topaz Glas-O-Past-X.

Thin the color as needed with acetone. Let the paint dry.
Pick up the copper screen with tweezers and hold it under running water to rinse off the sodium bisulphate. Also rinse the spots under the tweezer tips.
Dry the screen between two cloths and lay it in a warm place. Hereafter, do not touch the screen again with your fingertips.
Cover the screen with some unthinned, transparent yellow Glas-O-Past-X.
Lay it in the middle of the practically dry glass plate.
Lay mosaic glass on the glass plate.
Lay both plates on the forming dish and heat the kiln to about 1463° F. (795° C.)—cone 016.

Illus. 61. This blue plate has leaf motifs made of enclosed glass grit. By Mevrouw Meyling-de Kat.

49

A GLASS RELIEF

The most striking of the Glas-O-Past-X colors are the very brilliant ones, including both opaque and transparent pigments. When you paint with these colors, you will be especially disappointed if your work cracks upon cooling. Although this does not happen very often, when it does, as mentioned earlier, improper work methods are always to blame, though it is often difficult afterwards to say precisely where the mistake lay.

Don't throw cracked dishes away, however. Hang on to them and use them for making glass reliefs. For this purpose, have the glass dealer cut a piece of reinforced wire-glass for you (this is glass strengthened with a metal mesh) and treat it in the usual way. That is to say, file the edges round, clean it, and so on. Cover this glass with a reasonably thick layer of transparent pigment in a light tint, leaving the edges rather free of color. Light yellow or lime green are suitable colors. Let this layer dry quite thoroughly. (Thinning with acetone is therefore recommended, as acetone dries quickly.)

Now take a piece of swanskin (a thin, soft cloth), or an old piece of flannel or other thick, soft cloth and lay the cracked dish in the middle of it with the bulge on top. With the rounded side of a rubber mallet, smash the dish into pieces. The pieces must not be too small, averaging about 2″ to 2½″ across, with some pieces a little smaller and others a little larger. Along the edges, lay down a trail of gum arabic or epoxy cement. Next, bend two hanger-eyes from heavy-gauge nickel-silver wire and lay them on the plate. Now lay the plate on the separator-coated kiln shelf and place upon it the pieces of glass with their bulged sides upwards and overlapping each other in the manner of roof shingles. Take special care that small pieces of glass cover the hanger-eyes, so that these can be melted in firmly.

Next, place the kiln shelf in the kiln and take care in doing so that the pieces of glass are not moved out of place so as to overhang the edge. Bring the kiln temperature up very slowly and heat the glass to about 1481° F. (805° C.)—cone 015.

This very thick wall relief must now cool off for an exceptionally long time. Since you have used different kinds of glass in its composition, there will be a difference in the internal strains of the different pieces, so that crackle-type cracks will appear in the under layer, allowing a splendid show of transmitted light. Only rarely will you be sorry about a cracked dish!

Checklist for Making a Glass Relief:
Cut a piece of wire-mesh-reinforced glass. File off the sharp edges as well as the sharp, metal points sticking out. Clean with denatured alcohol. Cover the glass plate with a coat of transparent paint thinned with acetone. Fold an old cloth around the cracked glass dish and strike it on the bulging side with a rubber hammer or with the ball side of a ball-peen hammer. File the glass fragments only on the edges of the bulging side.

Lay out the pieces of glass so that they overlap like shingles.
On top of these, lay the smaller pieces of the shattered dish.
Fill empty spaces with transparent, mosaic glass.
Place the glass in the kiln.
Heat the kiln slowly to about 1481° F. (805° C.)—cone 015.
Let kiln and contents cool off thoroughly before opening.

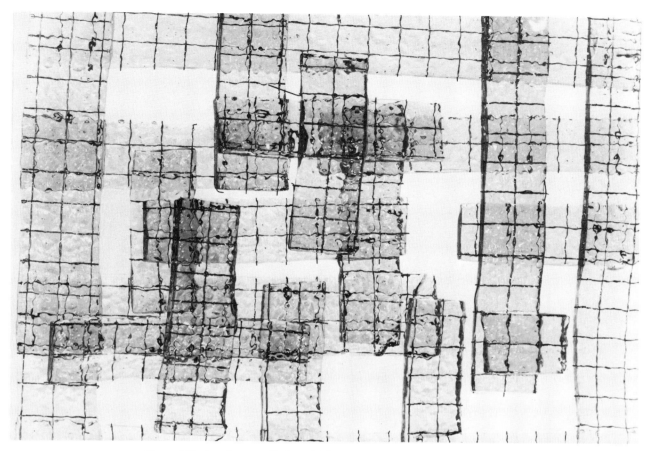
Illus. 62. A glass relief, utilizing reinforced wire-glass.

FROSTING GLASS

Thus far you have worked with ordinary, transparent glass. However, you can also make very attractive pieces out of textured glass, but this kind of glass is less easy to cut. You can have the glass dealer cut it for you with his circle cutter and, at the same time, ask him for the waste pieces. The pieces you can use are much smaller than those the glazier uses for glazing even the smallest pane. Generally, he will never be able to use the kind of pieces you will find so useful. Most textured glass will fire to transparency.

Frosted glass creates a totally different effect, because it is translucent rather than transparent.

You can frost decorated, transparent glass by avoiding drying the layer of separator before firing the glass in the kiln. The moisture released from the coating by the heat works its way into the glass and frosts it. Do not use large kiln shelves for this treatment, because they may crack.

Checklist for Frosting Glass:
Cut glass to the desired size. File the edges until they feel smooth.
Decorate the glass with different colors of Glas-O-

Past-X. Coat the kiln shelf or forming dish with separator but do not let the coating dry.
Lay the glass on the form or shelf and bring the kiln temperature up quickly.

52

GLASS COSTUME JEWELRY

To make a necklace, you can use small squares or oblongs of glass, color them with Glas-O-Past-X and enclose (or leave them plain) small pieces of material such as fine copper screen, glass mosaic, and so on.

Round, triangular, and other shapes may also be used, and not all the pieces need have the same shape or size. The main thing is that you must mount on the upper side two hanger-eyelets of nickel-silver wire, enclosing them between the two glass plates. For example, lay a rectangular piece of glass on a round glass plate, or lay one oblong piece across another in such a way that the middle of the top piece covers the upper end of the other, where the eyelets are located. The finished piece results in a doubled part at the top, while the "wings" at the sides and the extension beneath are single thicknesses of glass.

The possibilities are practically unlimited, and the results can be very exciting. Remember, too, that when they are being worn, glass necklaces take on the color of the clothing worn beneath, so that a single necklace will change color and become different with each change of costume. For example, blue, transparent glass on a yellow background appears greenish; on grey, dark blue, and so on. The true color of the glass is visible only when it is worn over white. This does not, however, hold true for the opaque colors of Glas-O-Past-X.

You can make bracelets by melting links of nickel-silver chain into both sides of the glass pieces and, after firing, connecting them together.

Checklist for Making Glass Jewelry:
With the glass pliers, cut a large number of small pieces of glass.
File the edges of the fragments very smooth and rounded.
Always combine two or three pieces in a single unit of a necklace.
Cover the bottom layer with Glas-O-Past-X, then lay on a piece of mosaic glass, silver foil, some mica flakes, copper screen, copper filings, and so on.
Bend hanger-eyelets from light-gauge nickel-silver wire and lay these on the decorated glass plate.
On top of this, place one or more glass fragments, making sure that the hanger-eyelets are well covered. Other parts do not have to be covered completely, except where an enclosure is involved. Mosaic glass will stick naturally and so can be placed on the outside.
Lay all the parts on a prepared kiln shelf.
Check to make sure that the glass has not been displaced in handling and that the hanger-eyelets are covered with the glass.
Let the hanger-eyelet stick out at least $\frac{1}{4}''$, for in melting round, the glass manages to thrust a little outwards.
Heat the glass to cone 015.

Illus. 63. (Opposite). This stunning necklace is made of strips of ribbed glass with orange, white, and dark blue colored pieces of mosaic glass enclosed. The mounting is made of heavy nickel-silver wire.

MAKING BEADS FROM GLASS TUBING

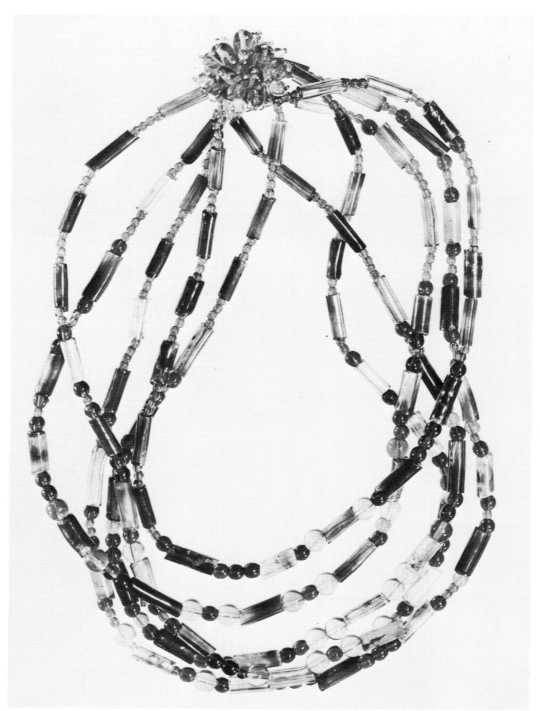

When you start to assemble a necklace, linking the parts together with nickel-silver wire hooked into the hanger-eyes, it may occur to you that a few beads placed between the necklace segments will provide just the right amount of added charm. You can buy beads

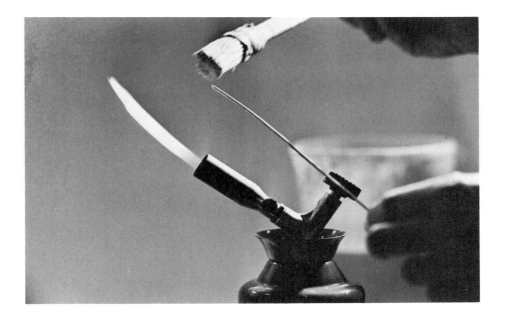

Illus. 65. First, coat the end of a knitting needle with separator and dry it over the flame.

especially for this purpose, or you can make them yourself with the help of a Bunsen burner. You can also use a propane gas torch, which is available at every hardware dealer's.

To make the beads, first cut and break with glass-cutting pliers a length of glass tubing into short pieces. Glass tubing is laboratory glass and is very inexpensive. It is sold by weight. Snip off a whole bowlful of pieces. On the left of the Bunsen burner (or torch), which should be resting on a sheet of asbestos or firebrick, place a jar filled with fluid separator. Fill another with clean water and place it to the right of the burner. Also place nearby a tube or two of transparent Glas-O-Past-X.

With a pointed brush, coat the end of a slim knitting needle with separator and dry it over the flame. Then slip the point of the needle into a piece of glass tubing and hold this in the flame until it begins to glow and the broken edges become somewhat rounded.

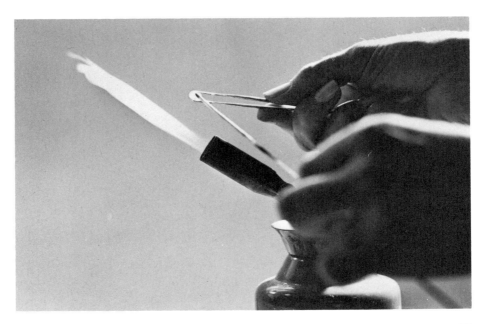

Illus. 66. Slip the point of the needle into a piece of glass tubing.

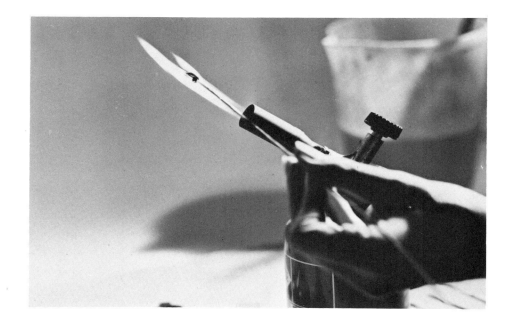

Illus. 67. Hold the tubing in the flame until the edges round off slightly.

Drop the bead on the asbestos sheet to cool and thrust the hot knitting needle into the jar of cold water. The separator lets go immediately, popping off in the water. Dry the point on a rag and re-coat it, and continue as before with another piece of glass tubing. When you have the right number of beads ready, press a small quantity of pigment out of a tube and thin it a little, but no more than enough to make it spread smoothly. Color each bead with paint while it is held on the separator-covered knitting needle, then hold it a short distance from the flame until it dries. Move it slowly towards the flame while turning it to equalize the heat all over. The paint will start to bubble a little, and then will flow out smoothly.

Illus. 68. Drop the bead on an asbestos mat to cool.

Illus. 69. Dip the needle into cold water until the separator pops off.

Since the gas flame brings about a reduction of the oxygen available to the hot paint, do not expect the same color you would get if firing in an electric kiln. Blue stays pretty much the same, but the other colors tend towards a greenish hue of about the same tone found in very old bottles, and varying from light to a very dark green. Transparent colors, on the other hand, when melted in the flame of a Bunsen burner, harmonize beautifully with each other, and you can assemble very handsome strings of these beads. Opaque colors, though, do not do as well. Glass tubing is also available which melts so quickly that the pieces can be rounded and colored in the heat at the same time.

If you want to use opaque colors in making beads, you must fire them in the kiln, and

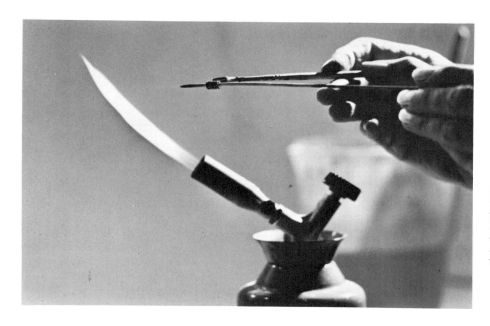

Illus. 70. When the beads are ready, paint them with Glas-O-Past-X while holding them on the knitting needle, and then dry close to the flame.

for this you must use a special holder, called a "porcupine." Shape a small bowl out of grogged clay, turn it upside-down and, while the clay is still wet, poke it full of 4″ lengths of Nichrome wire, letting them project in all directions.

Let the porcupine dry and fire it in the kiln to biscuit temperature for the clay you are using (the dealer from whom you bought it can tell you what its biscuit-fire temperature is).

After the fired porcupine has cooled, it is ready for use. Paint the Nichrome wires with separator, color the beads and stick one on each wire, taking care that the beads do not touch each other, or else they will stick together. Since Nichrome wire stays pliable, you can easily bend the wires apart where necessary. Set the bead-covered porcupine in the kiln and heat it to cone 018, which is 1328° F. (720° C.).

Mixing transparent colors with white pigment is recommended too for this purpose. They come out of the fire gleaming with opalescent tints.

As these beads have rather large holes through them, you can string them on nickel-silver wire. First take a few beads, then a hanger-eye from a glass segment, then another one or two beads and the second hanger eye, and again beads, and so on. Make the part that goes around in back of the neck out of two pieces of heavy-gauge nickel-silver wire, shaping the ends with a pliers into a hook-and-eye clasp (see Illus. 63).

Checklist for Making Beads:
Cut small pieces of glass tubing about ⅜″ long. (Use glass-cutting pliers.)
Set a jar of separator and a jar of cold water next to the Bunsen burner.
Find a thin, steel knitting needle that has room around it when passed through the glass tubing.
Light the Bunsen burner and adjust the flame until it stands very high.
Dip the knitting needle in separator and dry it in the flame.
Stick a piece of glass tubing on the knitting needle and let the edges round off a little in the flame.
Slip the bead off the knitting needle.
Stick the knitting needle in cold water to make the separator pop off, then dry it and coat it again with separator. Dry it in the flame.

Take up a bead on the knitting needle and brush a little thinned, transparent Glas-O-Past-X on it. Hold the bead 4″ from the tip of the flame to dry. Heat the glass either in the oxidizing or reducing part of the flame. (Hold the bead just above the tip of the visible flame, where it will be in a clear, blue, practically invisible, extension of the flame, called the oxidizing flame. If the bead is held lower, so as to be inside the luminous tip of the flame and above the core of unburned air and gases emerging from the burner, it is in a reducing flame.)
Let the paint melt and flow in the flame.
Slide the bead off on a piece of asbestos to cool.
Thrust the hot knitting needle into cold water.
Dip it again in separator and continue treating the beads until all are done.

Checklist for Making a "Porcupine":
Out of grogged clay make a little dish about 2″ high by 4″ across.
Let this get leather-hard (hard enough that you can no longer bend it).
Snip 20-gauge Nichrome wire into pieces 4″ long. Stick the wires into the clay, then let the porcupine dry throughly.

Fire to 1814°–1859° F. (990°—1015° C.)—cone 07 or 06.
Paint the porcupine's "needles" with separator. Place a bead on each wire and paint them one by one, as they are put on, with opaque or transparent paint.
Set the porcupine in the kiln; heat to 1328° F. (720° C.)—cone 018.

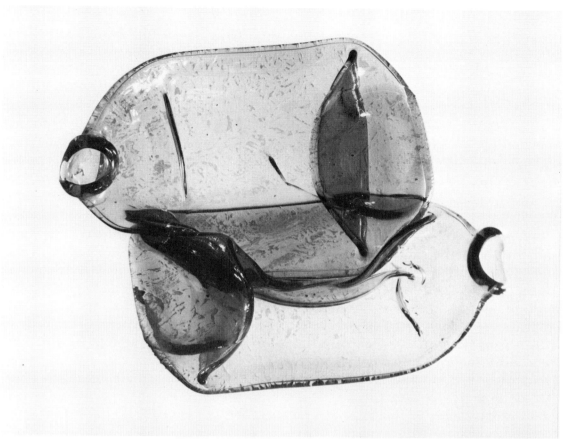

Illus. 71. A bottle ashtray.

WORKING WITH BOTTLES

As we said at the beginning, you would only work with uncolored glass to prevent damage to the kiln or kiln shelves. The only exception is bottle glass. Gather together all the colored bottles you can get your hands on, especially blue ones, which have a particularly lovely color which will be useful for many purposes.

Let's begin by making an ashtray out of two small green bottles without necks. (Certain headache tablets come in such bottles.) Paint with separator a forming dish that is not too deep but large enough to hold the bottles without having them project over the rim. Lay the bottles neck-to-bottom and side-by-side in the forming dish. If lettering or markings have been impressed into the glass, turn the marked side down so that the markings will be on the bottom of the ashtray. Fire to 1463° F. (795° C.)—cone 016.

Checklist for Making an Ashtray from Bottles:
Prepare a large forming dish that is not too deep.
Pour denatured alcohol into the bottles and shake them up until all dirt is dissolved off the inside of the glass. Pour out the alcohol and repeat with new. Clean the bottles on the outside with alcohol.
Lay the bottles side by side in the forming dish,
the neck end of one beside the bottom of the other, with all impressed markings on the bottom.
Rest necks and bottoms of the bottles directly under the rim of the forming dish.
Place in kiln and heat slowly to 1463° F. (795° C.) —cone 016.
Let kiln and contents cool off slowly.

59

Bottle Birds

You can have a lot of fun with bottles. Try this. Tie the neck of a bottle with Nichrome wire to a separator-coated shelf support in such a way that the bottle hangs on a diagonal, its bottom edge resting on the separator-covered kiln shelf. Lay a kiln shelf on top of the shelf support to give it added weight and to hold it against toppling over from the weight of the bottle.

When the glass is heated sufficiently, the bottle will lie down on the kiln shelf under it, the bottle neck stretching out to accommodate the change in position. Sometimes the neck will sag very low, so that it takes on the shape of a bird's head.

You can control this to a large extent. When the glow of the kiln begins to change to a brighter color, follow the process by watching through the peep-hole, so you can shut down the kiln at precisely the right moment.

Do not worry about after-radiation from the kiln shelves, for this would have a possible effect only on the bottle neck.

Once the glass has been heated until it is weakened, the neck will stretch out quite a lot from the weight of the bottle. The farther the neck is stretched, the more remarkable are the results you get.

Another method of melting bottles together is to set a bottle upright in the middle of the kiln shelf. Arrange a number of similar bottles around it in a ring, so that they touch each other, and bind them together with a very thin Nichrome wire.

Place the bottles in the kiln with the kiln shelf at such a height that the shoulders of the bottles come directly opposite the peep-hole.

When the kiln reaches its first glow at a temperature of about 1121°–1202° F. (605°–650° C.)—cone 022 to 020, keep a continual watch at the peep-hole in order to follow the process closely.

As soon as the bottle necks begin to bend and start twisting, switch off the kiln. Do not let the bottles soften too much, or they are likely to melt and flow off in a mass that can damage the kiln walls.

Checklist for Making Birds out of Bottles:
Cover a kiln shelf and a tall shelf support with separator.
Tie the neck of the bottle securely to the upper part of the shelf support with very thin Nichrome wire. Wrap the wire round the neck just under the collar. Repair if necessary the coating on the shelf support.

Also coat the Nichrome wire, except where it is wrapped round the bottle.
Raise the kiln temperature to about 1202° F. (650° C.)—cone 020 and thereafter keep a continual watch at the peep-hole.
When the bottle necks start to bend and twist, shut down the kiln.

Colorful Bottle-Glass Gems

Bottle glass is very useful for many purposes. One of these is the making of "gems." Use the thickest part of the bottle, which is the rim round the "kick" (the kick of a bottle is the indentation moulded in the bottom, and the thickest glass is found in the rim the bottle rests upon).

Bits of this heavy glass will, upon being exposed to the heat of the kiln, turn into large drops of molten glass.

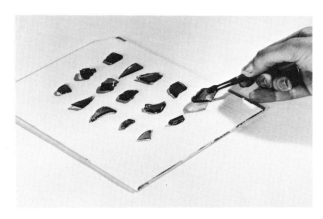

Illus. 72. The fragments of a green bottle are laid on a separator-coated shelf.

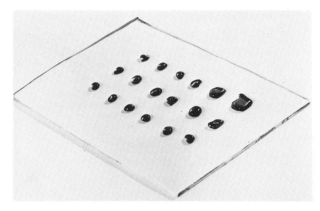

Illus. 73. After firing in the kiln, the fragments formed round shapes like cabochon gems.

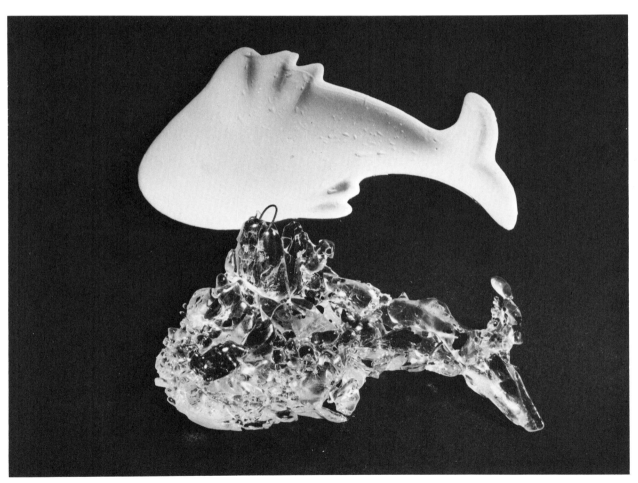

Illus. 74. The "gems" were then used to decorate this fish dish.

Before the glass flows outwards, surface tension pulls it inwards, into a ball-shape. The little pieces of glass thus form drops, which refract light into a deep color. Of course, the temperatures at which we have been working so far are not high enough to produce this effect. Therefore, once you have heated the kiln to about 1463° F. (795° C.)—cone 016, take up a post in front of the peep-hole and keep a sharp watch on proceedings; or, use an alarm clock or bell-timer to remind you at short intervals to take another look into the kiln. This way, you will be able to watch the glass turn into molten balls and judge when to shut down the kiln.

If you happen to be working with a large kiln, to avoid a waste of time as well as kiln space, make up a large number of fragments to turn into gems. You will find dozens of uses for them, so you cannot make too many. Break up bottles of all colors, and remember, too, that colorless bottles, which often have a pale blue look, and fragments of show-window glass or of jam jars, can also be used.

Because you use very small fragments in this method, you can also make tests with the kind of colored glass used in leaded window panes, commonly called "stained glass." In this case, separate the different colors of glass in the kiln and take up your post like a watchdog in front of the peep-hole. Where bottle glass is concerned, nearly all colors of glass assume a ball shape at the same time.

The fragments do not have to be round to begin with when you want to create round gems, since the corners round off in the heating process.

There are countless possibilities open to you in the use of these gems—you can set them into rings and costume jewelry, melt them into wall plaques, or stick them on hangers and vases in the form of glass mosaics.

To break down into small fragments, wrap the bottle in a piece of cloth large enough so that the bottle cannot roll out. Then throw the cloth-wrapped bottle forcibly against a concrete floor or sidewalk. Open and check for pieces that are too large. Strike these on the bulging side with a mallet, leaving the glass wrapped in the cloth to prevent scattering the pieces. Store the pieces in a can.

Next, wrap a second bottle in the cloth and treat it the same way until you have a large number of fragments in all different colors.

When finished, throw the cloth away or burn it. The fabric is filled with splinters which, if they get into your skin, will be difficult to remove.

Contraction of the glass in the kiln takes place in separate phases. First, the glass rounds off somewhat; then follows a complete rounding of the pieces with the top still flat. After this, the glass starts to bulge upwards, becoming smaller in breadth, but thicker. In general, use bits of glass measuring from $\frac{3}{8}''$ to $1\frac{1}{8}''$ in diameter—these are the most useful sizes.

Checklist for Making Glass Gems:
Coat several kiln shelves with separator. Let dry. Wrap a bottle in a cloth and throw it forcibly against a concrete floor. Sort out pieces that are too big and shatter them into smaller bits with the ball of a machinist's hammer. Open the cloth and shake the glass into a can.
Wrap another bottle in the cloth, and continue until you have a lot of pieces.

Lay the fragments one by one on the kiln shelf, handling them with tweezers. Leave about 1″ of space between pieces.
Heat the kiln quickly to 1463° F. (795° C.)—cone 016.
Sit in front of the kiln and watch the process through the peep-hole until every piece has melted into a ball shape. Shut off the kiln immediately. Burn or throw away the cloth.

CHRISTMAS ORNAMENTS

Collect a number of small bottles of various shapes. These can be decorated in many different ways and used for Christmas ornaments. Below are a number of suggestions, which you may develop further with ideas of your own.

Make sure that the bottles are good and dry on the inside before they undergo any work. Rinse out medicine bottles with water until they look clean. Drain the bottles, then pour in a little denatured alcohol and swish it around so as to contact every part of the inside, and then pour it out. Add a little fresh alcohol, do the same again, and pour it out. After this treatment, any water remaining in the bottle is so thoroughly mixed with alcohol that it quickly evaporates. Pour the used alcohol into a jar so that you can use it again for cleaning the outsides of the bottles. A bottle that has contained an oily substance can be properly cleaned only if it has a wide neck opening. It is often difficult to clean the bottle thoroughly through a narrow neck and, when the oily residue goes through the fire, the gases generated cannot escape and so cause the glass to bulge until it shatters.

However, it is different when you enclose air in the glass on purpose to cause it to bulge out, which is exactly what you will do. Following are several different kinds of Christmas ornaments.

1. Take a small medicine bottle and pour into it some medium green or red-purple Glas-O-Past-X mixed with acetone. Be sure that the paint coats the whole inside of the bottle. Pour out excess. Pour two or three drops of liquid gold (a metallic overglaze) into the bottle. Try as much as possible to make the liquid gold spread out on the surface of the paint.

In a glass marble, with the sharp corner of the carborundum stone, file two small grooves directly opposite each other. Bend a long loop from light-gauge nickel-silver wire for hanging on your tree. Paint the neck of the bottle with Glas-O-Past-X. With one hand, stick the wire loop a little way into the bottle neck, and set the glass marble on top of the neck, making sure that the wires fit nicely into the grooves filed into it. Brush more color along the joints. Place the bottle on a prepared kiln shelf where it can be seen through the kiln peep-hole and let the kiln heat up until the glass is bulged to your satisfaction. The marble will retain air, allowing the glass to bulge. Do not let it bulge out too far, or the Christmas ball will fall over in the kiln.

2. Thoroughly clean a small flat bottle inside and out with alcohol. Lay the bottle down flat on its side, for when the glass softens, the bottom will collapse and bend over. Choose glass mosaic pieces or "gem stones" of glass in different colors and sizes. Brush a thin layer

of glass or enamel glue on the flat side of the bottle. Measure the width of the bottom, and lay the mosaic pieces in a design on the bottle to just above the line on the bottle where the bottom will come when it folds over. Bend a loop of nickel-silver wire and lay this in the neck for a hanger. Lay the bottle (several bottles can, of course, be fired at the same time) on the kiln shelf, which has been painted with separator. Heat the kiln to the usual temperature. Let it cool off slowly.

3. Clean a round bottle inside and out with alcohol. Drip a little Glas-O-Past-X thinned with acetone into it. Cover the inside of the bottle with paint by turning it around in your hands. Keep turning the bottle until the paint becomes thicker. Shake a few coarse mica flakes into the bottle and add a few small glass beads. Bend nickel-silver wire into a long, narrow rectangle, so that the width is narrow enough to slip easily through the neck of the bottle. Push the wire rectangle a short distance into the bottle, making sure that the free ends of the wire are inside the bottle and the closed end forms a hanging loop outside. Otherwise, the unclosed loop will straighten out when you hang up the Christmas ornament. Lay the bottle on a prepared kiln shelf and heat the kiln to the usual temperature. Let cool.

4. Clean an uncolored bottle inside and out. Bend a large loop of nickel-silver wire and stick the free ends into the bottle until they touch the bottom, so that a large hanger-eye still projects from the bottle neck. Fill to within $\frac{5}{8}''$ of the neck with colored glass grit. Fire the bottle standing, until the neck sags in.

5. Fire the same bottle, lying on its side.

6. Select a flat bottle that has a circular shape in the vertical plane. Coat the inside with medium-green transparent paint. On the prepared kiln shelf lay a star of glass points coated on their upper sides with liquid gold, but do not paint them all the way in to the middle. Bend a long loop of nickel-silver wire and place it in the bottle neck, looped end out. Lay the bottle in the middle of the star. Lay blue-green, dark green, and honey yellow mosaic pieces in a star shape on the flat side of the bottle. Heat the kiln to the usual temperature. Let cool.

7. Lay a bottle on the same star of golden points, which is set up on the kiln shelf. Lay a smaller star of colored points on the flat side of the bottle. Hold the star securely in the middle by laying on it, upside-down, a glass stopper from a small, stoppered bottle. Fire and let cool.

8. Cut points out of a piece of broken show-window glass. Cut a plate of wire-reinforced glass about 4″ square. Lay this plate on a prepared kiln shelf. Bend a long loop of nickel-silver wire and lay this diagonally across the wire-glass. Color the points of the show-window glass on the upper side with alternate layers of transparent and opaque Glas-O-Past-X.

Cover the wire-glass with a layer of transparent paint. Lay the points with their painted sides up on the wire glass. In the middle, lay a square of show-window glass and coat it with liquid gold. Heat the kiln to 1292° F. (700° C.)—close to cone 018, or 1328° F. (720° C.).

A collage made of various kinds of broken glass, including bottles, colored and melted together with inclusions of metal.

This wall collage is composed of wire-glass, pieces of broken aquarium glass, and a few pieces of copper. The large blue element is a shampoo jar which was placed in the kiln directly in front of the peep-hole so it could be watched carefully. As soon as the screw-thread vanished, the kiln was shut down.

J

Here is a Christmas tree that will last forever! For complete directions on how to make it, see page 66.

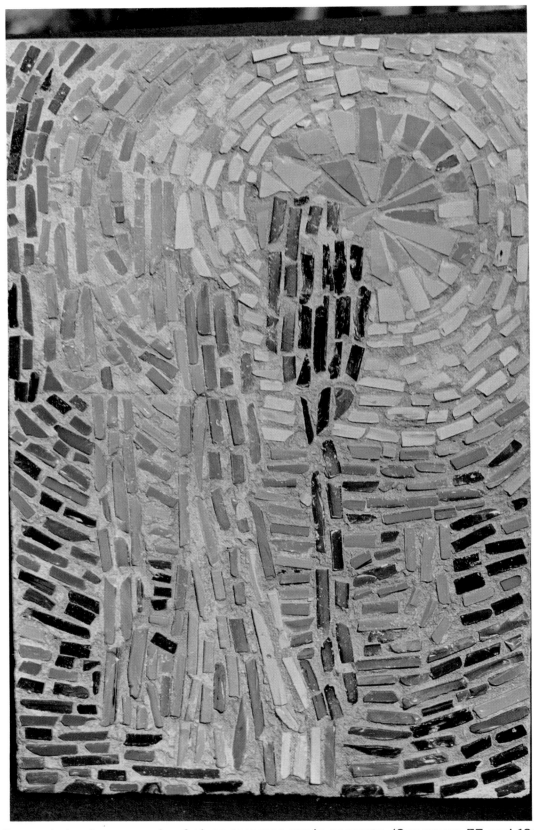

A mosaic landscape made of glass tesserae set in concrete. (See pages 77 and 104.)

This wall plaque is made of shards of heavy construction glass and a piece of wire-reinforced glass. Enclosed are mica flakes. Opaque turquoise and white Glas-O-Past-X were used for coloring.

If you want a bottle neck to fold over like this in the kiln, you should cut it off on an angle.

N

This bottle neck did not fold over because it was cut straight. However, if you lay the collage on an angle in the kiln, the neck will bend.

Pendants, charms, rings and other pieces of your own glass jewelry, colored with Glas-O-Past-X will be the envy of your friends. You'll never see these in a jewelry shop. Every piece you make will be uniquely yours.

Illus. 75. A unique Glas-O-Past-X-colored glass wind chimes. By Monica van Vlijmen.

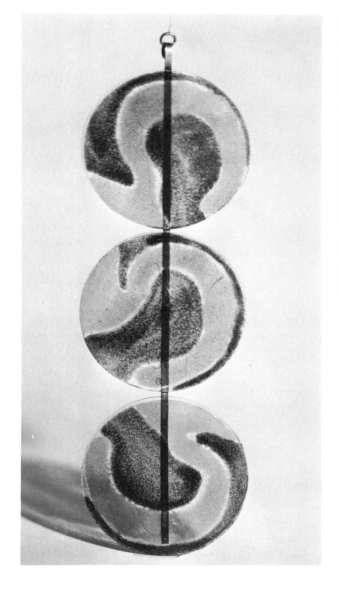

Illus. 76. A unique hanging made of three Glas-O-Past-X-colored plates joined together by flat nickel-silver wire.

A CHRISTMAS

TREE

Illus. 77. See this colorful tree on color page K.

When a window-pane breaks, it is generally because a misdirected ball or similar object has been thrown against it. However unfortunate that may be, you can turn some of the grief into joy by using the resulting fragments.

Usually, such a break occurs in a star shape, that is, the break-lines radiate from the point of contact with the shattering object. Thus, the glass falls in sharp points out of the window frame. Carefully preserve these points, because you can turn them into a Christmas tree! File all the glass points you have on hand. The lowermost points on the Christmas tree in Illus. 77 are 4″ to 5″ long. All told, 76 glass points were used in making the tree. Since you would scarcely get that many points out of one broken pane, you will have to cut as many more as you need. You can cut these out of glass strips by cutting each strip on a diagonal, thus getting two points at one stroke.

Make sure you have on hand some heavy-gauge nickel-silver wire. Prepare all the kiln shelves you have available. Unless you have a very large kiln, you will not be able to fire all the points at one time, unless, of course, you intend to make a very small tree in a small kiln.

Remember, in cutting the glass points, avoid making them all the same size. The more uneven they are, the more charm your tree will have. In coloring the tree, you will see how much the development of the color depends on how the glass pieces are put together. Wherever the glass is doubled, the color development is completely different from those

66

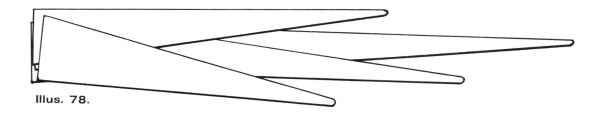

Illus. 78.

places where the color simply lies on top of one piece of glass. These differentiations of color can have handsome results.

Medium green is used in Illus. 77 which turned some of the glass assemblies towards turquoise-green where the paint was sandwiched between two pieces of glass. You, however, could just as well use transparent dark green. Wherever you double the glass, with Glas-O-Past-X between, the color will be pure blue; where the glass is single, deep dark green. In both cases, one Glas-O-Past-X color is sufficient to bring about several nuances of color.

Clean the glass thoroughly and lay all the filed and cleaned points in a box. Pick out a number of colored glass mosaic pieces, and a smaller number of uncolored ones.

Now, since this is a fairly long project, let's go step by step. Hunt up as many suitable glass points as you can find in the box and cut as many more as you need to make a total of nine groups of four double points. (This in total is 72 points.) You will also need four points for the peak of the tree. Make sure you have filed all points nice and smooth, and cleaned the glass thoroughly with alcohol. Lay four glass points one above the other on the kiln shelf, each consecutive point being smaller than the one below it, with a separation of about 1″ to 1¼″ between each point of glass. Coat the points with Glas-O-Past-X, taking special care to keep the paint from running over the edges.

Cut off a length of heavy-gauge nickel-silver wire. (Heavy Nichrome wire will also do.) Straighten it out. Lay the wire on the glass points, connecting them together so they are placed about ¾″ from the outer edge of the widest end of each piece of glass, and so that at least 3″ of wire are projecting below the lowermost glass point. Then lay a small number of glass mosaic pieces on each point. Bend hanger-eyes from light-gauge nickel-silver wire. Lay these on the lower edge of the narrow end points, one to two eyes per point for hanging "ornaments." Now take four more glass points and lay these on the wire and the glass. Take care that the points, which are now double, do not fit each other precisely. Make a total of 9 strips. If you have laid one series of these "branches" pointing to the right, lay another series pointing towards the left, or vice versa. In a large, polygonal kiln, you can lay two strips on one shelf.

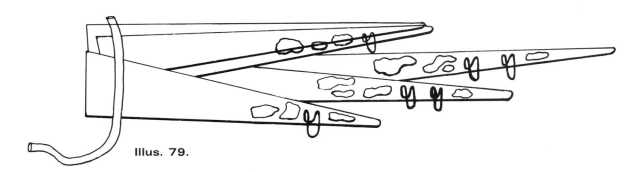

Illus. 79.

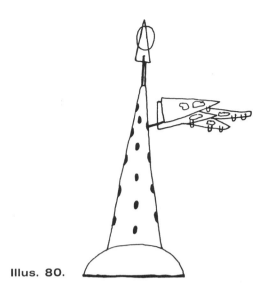

Illus. 80.

Now, to make the peak of the tree, cut off two pieces of nickel-silver wire and bend them straight. Place two glass points together in whatever position you would like them. Lay the end of the nickel-silver wire on the glass and cover with a second piece of glass. Repeat this to make the second point which is next mounted back to back against the first. Lay one or two glass mosaic pieces on each of the topmost glass points. Heat the kiln to the usual temperature. Let the kiln cool off thoroughly before opening.

Then, make the trunk of the tree. From dark clay mixed with grog, make a small, wide-topped form, similar to an unscooped-out bowl. Let it become leather-hard. Turn it upside-down on the table. Mould a long, thin peak on it, so it looks like a dunce cap. With a thick knitting needle, make a deep hole in the top of it, about 4″ deep. Make nine holes around this peak, from top to bottom, poking the needle all the way through. Let it get thoroughly dry; then, fire to the maturing temperature of the clay.

In order to assemble the tree, take a glass strip, and stick the projecting wire into one of the holes on the "trunk." With florists' binding twine, tie the nickel-silver wire to the earthenware. Do this with all the strips of glass. Then, tie all the strips together round the trunk to hold them firmly in place. Wind the free ends of the twine round the nickel-silver wire and stick them down with tape. Set the two points for the peak in the top hole.

Decorations for the Christmas Tree

Cut some very small triangles out of glass and color them with a thin coating of Glas-O-Past-X. Lay them on the prepared kiln shelf. Bend an equal number of hanger-eyes from thin, nickel-silver wire. Lay the hanger-eyes on the glass, then lay a second glass triangle on top. Fire the triangles to about 1481° F. (805° C.)—cone 015. After the triangles have cooled, paint them on one side with liquid gold. Place them in the kiln again and fire them to 1202° F. (650° C.)—cone 020.

Bend open the small connecting rings with a small pair of pliers or tweezers, and connect them to the hanger-eyes in the tree with the decorations; then, close the connecting rings with the pliers.

ENCLOSING PLANTS IN GLASS

Up to now, you have enclosed only non-combustible material, and considering the high temperature to which the glass is fired, you would think this would be the only kind of material you could use. Not so!

When wood burns, the ashes remaining consist largely of quartz, some alkalies, a small quantity of magnesium, some lime, a bit of iron, and other elements. These are materials that cannot be burned away. If plants are exposed to high heat, they will form the same kind of ashes—naturally in a smaller concentration than if wood were burned—but in sufficient quantity for your purposes. Flowers and leaves contain less permanent material than the stems, seed pods and seeds, although this varies according to the kind of plant. For instance, hard leaves such as holly, rhododendron, or fir needles, possess more permanent material than the leaves of a chrysanthemum; leaves of trees more than grasses, and grasses more than herbaceous plants. So, make a walking tour through your garden or nearby country area and select a number of plant parts to experiment with.

To begin with, select a modest number. You really do not need much for your first tests.

Illus. 81. This square dish was shaped in a round forming dish. A twig from a dried plant was painted with black Glas-O-Past-X and enclosed between two pieces of glass. The twig burned away, leaving a hazy skeleton behind it.

Pick up some lush grasses and a sprig of fir needles, and don't forget to gather a few dry needles from the ground. A few berries and leaves of holly, or some mountain ash berries, a few little rose hips, and you have a treasure trove.

Regardless of your intention, you probably picked more than necessary, so slip part of your take between the leaves of a book to dry and press, or, you can hang some plants up to dry. Set the greens aside in a jar of water, for wilted plants will not look as attractive as fresh ones, even after firing.

In the first test you make, cover the bottom glass plate with a heavily thinned layer of transparent Glas-O-Past-X. All the colors become much lighter in tone when heavily thinned. Smoky topaz is a very suitable color but lime green and light yellow are also satisfactory.

Thin the paint with acetone and let the glass plate dry. Then make a simple arrangement of a few plant parts. Snip off any sprigs or whatever that project beyond the edges of the plate on which you lay the arrangement. Then lay a second glass plate on top and weight it down with a couple of heavy books or similar objects. Leave it like that until the next day. Then, in the usual way, fire the glass to about 1418° F. (770° C.)—cone 017. After cooling, the plant elements will appear as a lightly tinted, hazy silhouette delicately painted on the glass. The shape appears to have remained intact and each kind of plant seems to show its own soft tint.

The color development of plants depends on the kind of plant it is as well as on the type of soil in which it was grown. A plant grown in soil strongly impregnated with iron will develop a soft brown color. If, however, lime is present in the ground, as well as iron, another kind of plant growth will be found, and the color resulting from the fire is often light yellow. Other plants create a white ash, but in any case, the plants will always develop a pastel tint of color in the fire. Such experiments will provide you with endless surprises.

There are other possibilities in using plants. Try setting a few full-grown herbaceous plants overnight in water in which copper- or cobalt-salts have been dissolved. Just as plants draw iron out of the soil, these plants must take up the metallic salts. (If you find metallic salts unavailable, try using carbonates of the color oxides. Nickel and manganese can be considered for these plant treatments. This is not unnatural as all these elements are present in the ground, though naturally in lighter concentrations.)

Remember that living plants provide a more intense color development than dried plants. Of course, you can treat dried plant stems with Glas-O-Past-X, in which case you can fire the glass to the usual temperature of 1463° F. (795° C.)—cone 016. During the firing, the Glas-O-Past-X dissolves the plant ashes and more space is created between the two glass plates, owing to the evaporation and burning out of the medium. Also, you can treat the harder leaves in the same way with liquid gold.

For those of you who live near a beach, try a test with seaweeds. They are especially decorative and contain a lot of minerals. Use them in combination with green paints, and don't be surprised if they come out blue.

Suggestions for Melting-in Parts of Plants

1. Collect plant parts, grasses, tiny twigs, seed pods, hard leaves, etc. File a rectangular glass plate smooth and round on all four edges. Clean the glass thoroughly. Do the same with a second plate of glass the same size. Cover one glass plate with thinned Glas-O-Past-X; start with smoky topaz. Let the paint dry. Lay a few lush grass blades on the glass. Snip off parts that stick out too far. Lay the second glass plate on the plants. Weight the assembly

with several books on top. Let sit until the following day; then fire the glass to about 1418° F. (770° C.)—cone 017.

2. Do another the same way, but this time fire the glass immediately.

3. Set the plants you have gathered overnight with their stems in a solution of a metallic salt, for example, copper nitrate, iron chloride, and so on. You can get metallic salts in small quantities at a drug store or chemical supply house. (If you are a ceramist, and, there-

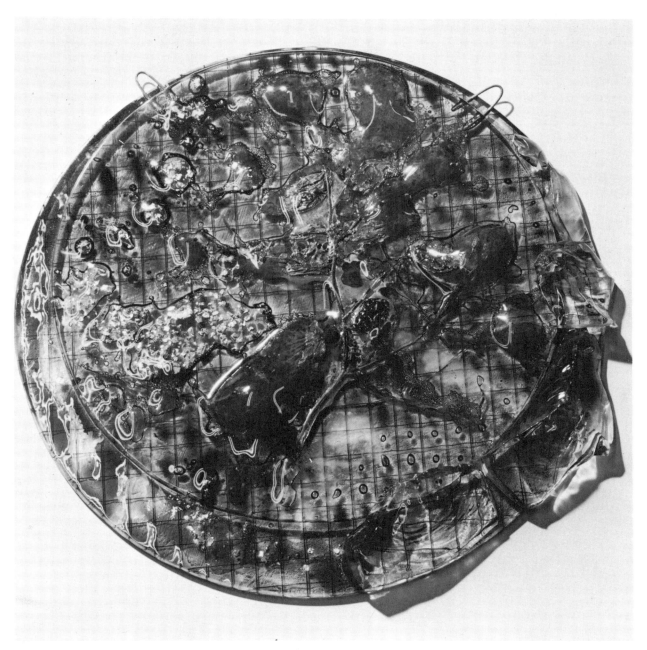

Illus. 82. This large, round plaque is made of a piece of wire-reinforced glass, covered with transparent Glas-O-Past-X. A twig was laid on the paint and covered with a piece of non-reinforced glass and fired.

fore, have various color oxides and carbonates at your disposal, make tests with them.) After filing the edges smooth, clean the glass and cover it with a neutral color of Glas-O-Past-X. Lay the plant parts on it. Heat to 1463° F. (795° C.)—cone 016.

4. Select a number of hard leaves that are not too big, say, a small sprig of holly. Coat the leaves with liquid gold. Let dry 24 hours. Cover the bottom plate with a lightly thinned coat of transparent Glas-O-Past-X in blue or medium green. Let these paints get thoroughly dry. Then, lay the sprig of holly on the glass. Lay another glass plate on top of the holly. Fire the glass to 1139° F. (615° C.)—cone 021.

5. Coat a glass plate with as even a thickness of Glas-O-Past-X as possible, in deep turquoise color. Let it dry a little. Select a number of limp leaves from some herbaceous plants or ferns. Paint them with liquid gold. Lay them painted-side down on the second glass plate and make an attractive composition of them. The liquid gold will cause the leaves to stick to the glass. Turn the second glass plate over and lay it on the colored under-glass, so that the leaves are sandwiched between the two glass plates. Heat to 1139° F. (615° C.)—cone 021.

6. Arrange a variety of seaweeds on a well-cleaned, but uncolored, glass plate. If there are air bubbles on the seaweed, prick them with a needle to let the air out. Coat the second plate with medium green, transparent Glas-O-Past-X. Lay the plate colored-side up on the seaweed, trying not to disturb the arrangement. Heat the glass to 1463° F. (795°C.)—cone 016.

7. Cut two plates, each about 8″ square, from the translucent, rippled glass that is often used for glass doors. File the edges and clean thoroughly. Coat the stripes on the glossy, smooth side of the bottom plate with reddish purple, transparent paint. Lay the second plate on top in such a way that the stripes criss-cross those of the other plate. Take a thin twig of a dried plant and coat it with black Glas-O-Past-X. Lay the twig on the second glass plate. Fire the glass to 1463° F. (795° C.)—cone 016. The twig burns away, leaving its skeleton.

A Glass Dish Enclosing Plants

Squeeze a tube of white Glas-O-Past-X out upon a round, glass plate. Thin with half acetone and half paint thinner to a thin fluid. Run it all over the surface by tilting the glass this way and that. Take care, however, that the paint does not run over the edges, and if it does, wipe it off at once. Take a birch twig with several catkins on it, and paint the veins of the leaves with opaque, dark blue Glas-O-Past-X. Paint the twig itself the same color, and the catkins with opaque orange. Lay the twig on the round glass plate in such a way that the tip of the twig follows the curve of the plate and fill out the design with a few transparent mosaic glass pieces. Lay a second glass plate on the first one, and place both plates on a prepared forming dish of the same size.

Place in the kiln and heat slowly to 1463° F. (795° C.)—cone 016.

A GLASS

WALL

LAMP

SHADE

Illus. 83.

If you want to make a shade for a wall lamp, you can make one completely of glass, but you have to go about it differently. Thus far, you have used an unglazed dish to support the work in the kiln. Yet, it is not always necessary for you to use an earthenware dish. You could use one made of metal; however, the kind of metal dishes that can be used without trouble are few and far between. It is certainly true that you can coat a thick, metal plate with separator and shape flat pieces of glass on it. So, to make a wall lamp shade you can also use metal, not in the form of a metal plate, but as wire.

For this, buy a metal trivet for an electric iron of the type shown in Illus. 85. These are made of chromed metal and provide a safe resting place for the soleplate of the iron. By bending the trivet smartly in the middle, you suddenly have a framework on which you can bend glass quite nicely.

The wires making up the trivet lie close enough together that the heat-softened glass will not penetrate between them.

When a flat, glass plate is laid on such a metal trivet and decorated on the upper side, the glass will accommodate itself to the bend of the trivet and assume a slightly wavy shape. The bend determines the shape of the lamp shade.

To avoid cracks in the glass, you might use wire-reinforced glass for such a piece. You can then apply designs with Glas-O-Past-X and glass fragments or chips. The metal must be first coated with separator. Place the piece directly in front of the peep-hole so you can see how the bending is getting along. Don't let it bend too much, however, or the glass will lose its strength and will crack as it cools. Also, do not lay glass chips and fragments too close to the edge of the glass, or the chips will slip right off the supporting plate. Always use a single glass plate. Sandwiched glass cracks because the bend is too sharp. Take care, too, that the glass plate is not wider than the trivet. If it should be wider, you can fire it

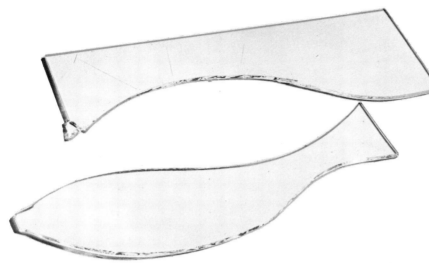

Illus. 84. The fish shape can easily be cut by making two curved lines on a single piece of glass and snapping off the excess as described on page 7.

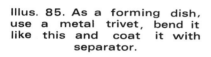

Illus. 85. As a forming dish, use a metal trivet, bend it like this and coat it with separator.

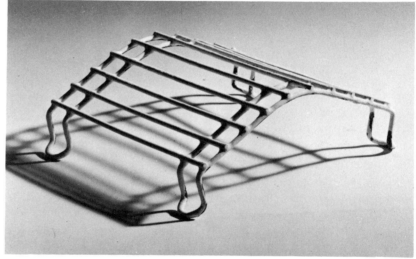

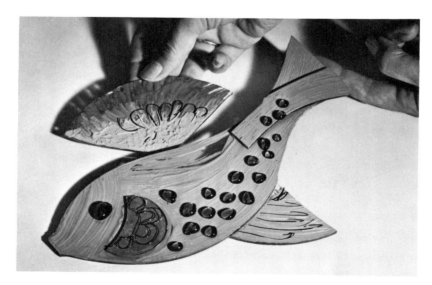

Illus. 86. Make the fins out of pieces of a round glass plate.

74

Illus. 87. Painting the last fin.

Illus. 88. Decorative pieces of wire are placed on the fins.

Illus. 89. Place the body of the fish carefully on the trivet so that it is balanced.

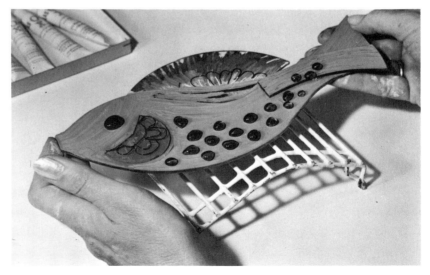

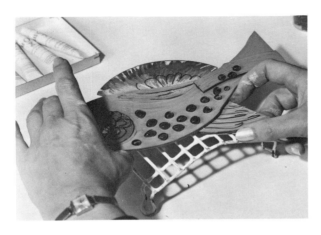

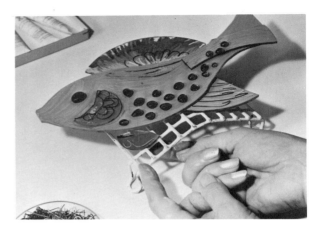

Illus. 90. Then lay on the fins underneath the body.

Illus. 91. The pieces will flow together when the glass begins to bend, so don't worry if they do not touch each other before firing.

anyway if you will support the middle of the overhanging glass plate on a prepared shelf support. The example in Illus. 83 was made this way.

Mount the glass with cement on a piece of nicely grained hardwood that can be fastened firmly to the wall, and attach the electrical equipment.

Checklist for Making a Wall Lamp Shade:
Buy a metal-wire, flat-iron trivet. Place it against a table edge and give it a quick bend in the middle. Brush a thick coating of separator on it.
Cut a piece of glass the same width as the trivet. The length is not important.
Decorate the glass with transparent Glas-O-Past-X and glass chips and fragments but not close to the ends that will bend down.

Prepare a kiln shelf and lay the trivet on it. Lay the glass plate exactly in the middle of the trivet.
Heat the kiln up to a temperature that produces a good glow. Then take your post at the peep-hole and wait until both sides of the glass have bent down equally. Shut down the kiln and let it cool off.
Cement the glass shade onto a piece of finished wood and attach electrical equipment.

MAKE A

MOSAIC

Illus. 92.

The word *mosaic* in its original sense refers to the joining together of small pieces of either natural stone or glass. Your mosaic will, of course, be made up of glass.

The most famous examples of glass mosaic are to be found in Italy—the still-glittering mosaics in Venice and in Ravenna—which are examples of mosaics composed of small slabs split off from thick plates of glass. These were set in mortar with the broken surface exposed. Because glass always shows a somewhat wavy surface at a break-line, the result is a considerable dispersion of the light falling on the mosaic. For this reason, stylized figures never appear to be stiff.

Flat glass laid in mortar always gives a stiff and awkward result, unless the craftsmanship of the artist executing the piece is so great, that even an improper use of the material cannot detract from its appearance. Antique mosaic glass was manufactured from a mixture of many kinds of basic materials, such as lead, quartz, lime, soda, potash, magnesium, kaolin, tin ashes, various color oxides, and so forth. So far as the composition is concerned, such material was much closer to being a glaze than real glass. There is one difference, though: The melting point of mosaic glass is considerably lower than that of glaze. (Remarkably, this antique glass, which was poured into moulds shaped like flat cakes, is still being manufactured in Germany. That is why you find such splendid glass mosaics on the façades of modern buildings in that country.)

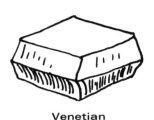

Venetian

Byzantine

Illus. 93. Nippers are best for cutting mosaic tesserae.

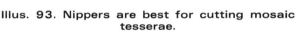

Safety goggles

There are two kinds of mosaic glass "tile" available to the craftsman. Venetian glass comes in $\frac{3}{4}'' \times \frac{3}{4}''$ pieces of quite smooth-sided glass which is either pasted on foot-square sheets of paper or in bulk form which is sold by weight. The color range is somewhat limited. Byzantine tile, which measures $\frac{3}{8}'' \times \frac{1}{2}''$ is made in large sheets which are machine split. Because it has irregular edges, it has higher reflective qualities. Sold in bulk, the range of colors is greater than that of Venetian glass tile.

Ready-to-mix cement for use with mosaic tile is available at all craft supply shops. Keep your mosaics fairly small, however, since cement of any kind is very heavy. In addition to your glass cutters, if you intend to cut up your tile pieces, a nippers just for that purpose is available. A word of caution when using nippers: *Always wear goggles.* The heavy pressure necessary for nipping the thick mosaic glass sends the pieces flying.

To make a mosaic, start by first making a wooden frame, and screw or nail a bottom of Masonite to it, smooth-side up. Make a paper cartoon of your design, and then mark out on the Masonite in rough lines the outlines of your design. Have a quantity of ready-mix cement on hand. Start by laying some of the ready-mix cement in one corner of the frame and press the bits of mosaic glass into the cement as you go, and follow your design until finished. Naturally, you can lay the pieces close against each other, but this is not necessary. Take care that no cement gets on the surface of the glass pieces. If it is left there to harden, it will be practically impossible to remove. Wipe the cement away with a damp cloth before it has a chance to harden, and do it immediately!

If you have to interrupt your work, prop up the frame on a slant so that the layer of cement slopes towards the bottom as sand slopes towards the sea. If you should leave a vertical separation and then the next day try to place fresh cement up against it, the surface would be too small for sticking the old and the new cement together satisfactorily. Your workpiece would probably break in two along that line as soon as you removed the frame. Make the sloping cement rough, to give a good tooth for the fresh cement to get a grip on. Of course, there are other kinds of filler material available which are satisfactory, but the ready-mix is easiest for the non-professional.

You might try another way to lay a mosaic. This is the classic "indirect" method. Lay a piece of carbon paper carbon-side up under a piece of heavy brown wrapping paper. Then draw your subject on the paper. Trace over it heavily so that your drawing appears in reverse on the back side of the wrapping paper. Turn the wrapping paper over and glue the mosaic pieces to the wrapping paper with *water-soluble glue.*

Next, make a frame, but substitute a piece of hard asbestos board for the Masonite. The bottom of the frame must be covered with a bed of mastic or mortar into which you press the glass pieces. Then, lay the paper with the tiles attached, paper-side up, onto the mastic or mortar bed.

Next, let the mastic harden for a few hours. In any case, do not let the material harden for *too short* a time before you turn it over, because if you break the plaque, you will never be able to repair it.

When you feel sure that the workpiece can be turned over, then the wrapping paper

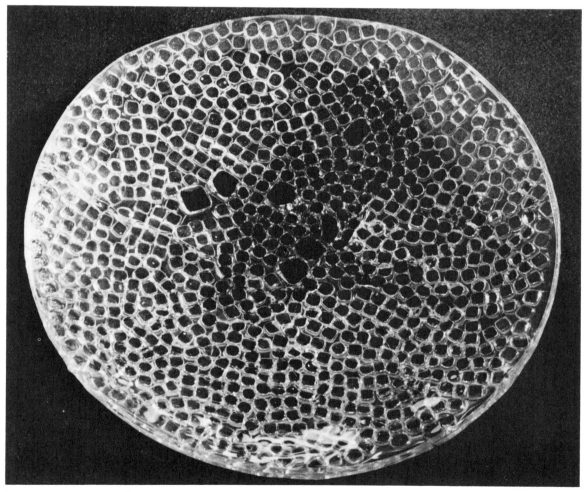

Illus. 94. Looking directly into a dish with enclosed tightly packed pieces of mosaic glass.

and glue must be removed. Do this by soaking the paper with water so that the glue will dissolve and let go. Peel the paper off. Then fill the spaces between the tiles with grout, a filler material available at craft houses. Use an old brush or rubber spatula. When finished, wipe the mosaic surface with a damp cloth to remove all glue and grout residue. Then wipe with a dry rag until the glass design glistens.

Checklist for Inlaying Mosaic Glass:

1. Make a rectangular frame of four laths (thin strips of wood) (1 × 2). Attach a Masonite bottom to the frame with screws or nails, being sure to have the rough side down and the smooth side inside the box. Turn the frame over so that it is like a flat box in front of you.

Sketch the design roughly on the board. Place a quantity of mosaic glass in a very shallow box. Have your glass nippers handy. Mix a small quantity of ready-mix mosaic cement. Fill a corner of the frame with cement. Carefully press the glass pieces into the cement, and, wherever possible, have the broken side up. Continue laying small areas of cement and glass. The cement dries quickly, so do not spread large areas at one time. Whenever you have to interrupt your work, slope the cement out on the bottom of the box. Scratch the surface to provide a good tooth for the fresh cement to cling to when you get around to resuming work. Remove all traces of cement from the mosaic pieces, before it has a chance to harden. Let set for several days and then remove the frame.

2. Take a piece of brown wrapping paper the same size as the mosaic you plan to make. Back it up with a piece of carbon paper turned so the carbon side is against the wrapping paper. Fasten the carbon paper on with a few paper clips. Draw the design on the wrapping paper. Remove the carbon paper and turn the wrapping paper over, so that the reversed tracing of the subject is up. Glue the mosaic pieces onto the paper with water-soluble glue. Measure the "paper" mosaic and construct a frame to accommodate it. Attach a thick ($\frac{1}{4}''$ to $\frac{3}{8}''$) sheet of hard asbestos board to the frame with screws or nails. Lay the paper, glass-side down onto the bottom which should be covered with a layer of mortar or mastic. Press in. Let it harden for a long time, preferably several days. Then, soak the wrapping paper and glue off the glass. Fill any spaces between the tiles with grout. Clean the surface of the glass mosaic pieces with a damp cloth.

Wipe with a dry cloth until the glass gleams. Then remove the frame.

Fired Mosaics

A new method of working this beautiful material of ancient composition is to fire it in the kiln until it softens. In this case, you do not have to use a filler.

It is important, when working in this way, that you use an abstract design, since the glass colors are subject to change when heated. In the case of an abstract mosaic, this is of less importance than where a naturalistic subject is concerned. You can lay out the mosaic directly on a prepared kiln shelf, and then heat the glass to a maximum of 1202°–1292° F. (650°–700° C.)—cone 020–019+. Make sure the pieces are in close contact with each other so they fuse together. Do not place a piece of window glass or wire-glass under the mosaic because the coefficient of expansion of mosaic glass is so different from that of ordinary glass because of its varied composition, that the mosaic would crack free of the underlayer. Heat it only to the point where the glass softens and sticks, and shut off the kiln. Let it cool completely.

Another method you might try is to heat to a higher temperature—cone 010–07+, but the procedure is different. First, glue the mosaic glass pieces to a sheet of wrapping paper. All over the prepared kiln shelf, shake dry separator through a sieve, making an even layer at least $\frac{3}{8}''$ thick. With a glass plate, press it down firmly, and then remove the glass. Make another layer with the powder, and press it down with the glass plate. Remove the plate. Then, lay the mosaic *paper-side down* directly on the dry coating of separator on the kiln shelf. The wrapping paper will burn out in the kiln without leaving any traces behind.

The colors at the higher temperature will have a strong tendency to change and, at the

Illus. 96. A lovely example of fired mosaic glass, displaying a unique craterlike texture.

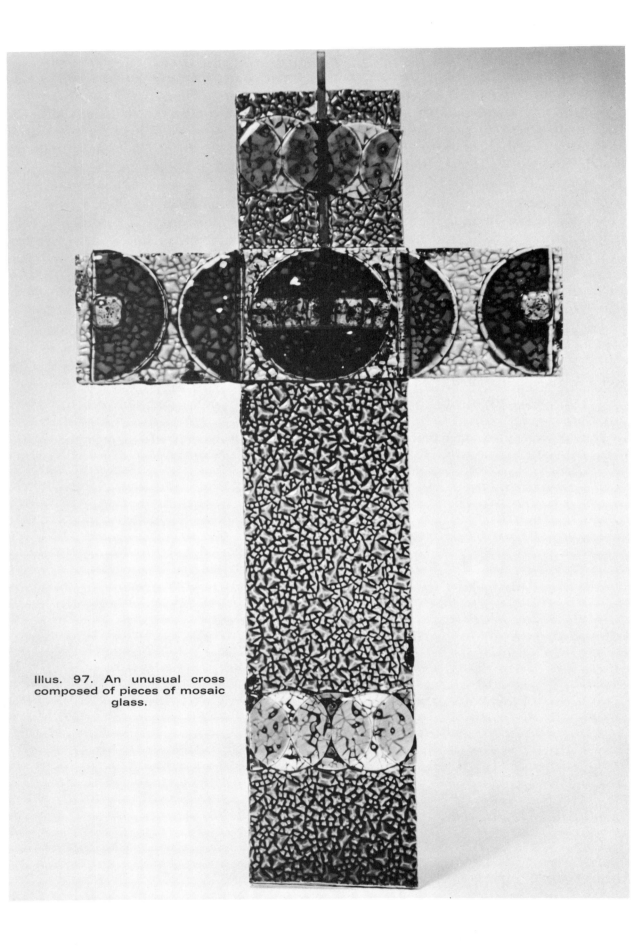

Illus. 97. An unusual cross composed of pieces of mosaic glass.

same time, will all run together, creating a lovely effect. Also, craterlike textures will form in the glass.

Another possibility is to fill a forming bowl all over the inside with a well-fitting layer of mosaic glass pieces. Prepare the forming dish beforehand with a poured-in coating of separator (see page 31). Heat the mosaic glass arrangement to a maximum of 1202°–1292°F. (650°–700° C.)—cone 020–019+.

The result will be an open-work dish which has a subtle mosaic character (see Illus. 98).

Checklist for Melting Glass Mosaic Pieces Together:
1. Prepare the kiln shelf. Assemble a mosaic directly on the kiln shelf, using pieces that fit well together. Fill any openings between the glass pieces with smaller fragments.
Place the mosaic in the kiln and heat slowly to 1202°–1292° F. (650°–700° C.)—cone 020–019+.
Let the kiln cool off slowly.
2. Prepare the kiln shelf. Spread a layer of dry separator $\frac{3}{8}$″ thick over it. Press the dry powder down with a glass plate. Spread a second layer of dry separator over the first and press it down with the glass plate. Remove the glass. Lay a piece of thick wrapping paper on the powdered kiln shelf, keeping it within about 2″ of the edge of the shelf all round. Assemble the mosaic pieces on the paper. (These do not have to fit together perfectly.) Place the mosaic in the kiln and heat to 1661°–1832° F. (905°–1000° C.)—cone 010–07+.
Let the kiln cool off slowly and thoroughly.

Dishes of Mosaic Glass and Glass Chips

Prepare a shallow forming dish. Apply a thicker layer of separator than normal. Lay the mosaic pieces side by side so that they fit as closely together as possible. Square mosaic pieces do not have sharp edges and are easier to work with. However, they do not have

Illus. 98. Here, pieces of mosaic glass were laid in a round forming dish and fired to form this open-work dish.

83

square edges; therefore, cover the forming dish with them in such a way that the glass will not slip out of position. The flatter the forming dish is, the easier it is to cover the inside with pieces of mosaic glass.

You can also use glass chips for lining the forming dish, preferably made from old bottles. Bottle glass has the advantage of not being as flat as ordinary glass and so has less of a tendency to slip. This makes it easy to place the glass in the forming dish. To make the right kind of chips for this, wrap the bottle in a cloth and throw it forcibly against a concrete floor. Use both colored and uncolored bottles. The different colors of glass can be combined, and you need not worry about differences in tension.

Never use Glas-O-Past-X in this method. The paint would penetrate through the glass and damage the coating of separator, and glass would then stick to the forming dish and both that dish and the workpiece would be ruined. Try making a clay form in the shape of a fish or bird (see color page A). Fill the form with glass chips and lay on eyes and other features in contrasting colors of mosaic glass. Fire to about 1292° F. (700° C.)— between cones 019 and 018.

If you want to hang the piece up, be sure to include a hanger-eye between pieces of glass.

Checklist for Making Dishes of Mosaic Pieces and Glass Chips:
Make a forming dish of clay, in the shape of a fish, a bird or some other animal.
Fire the clay to 1472° F. (800° C.)—between cones 016 and 015.
Pour separator into the form and pour it slowly out again, so that a thick layer remains.
Lay the pieces of glass chips in the form in such a way that it is completely covered with them.
If you want to hang the fish up, slip a hanger-eye between two of the larger pieces of glass.
Carefully place in the kiln, taking care that the pieces do not shift position.
Heat the kiln to about 1292° F. (700° C.).

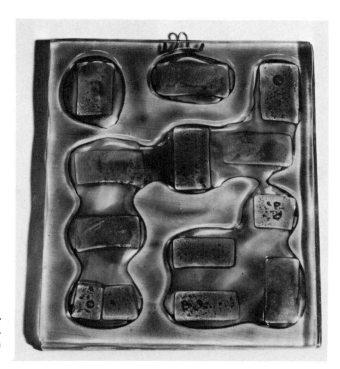

Illus. 99. Enclosed glass fragments with air bubbles resulting from placing the painted-side down create a subtle mosaic effect in this small plaque.

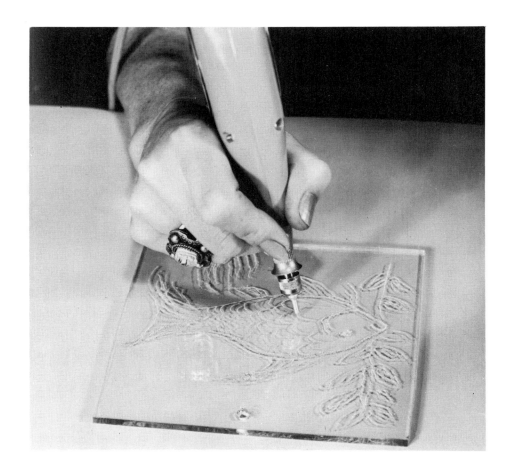

Illus. 100. Test your skill with the electric engraver first on flat pieces of glass.

ENGRAVING ON GLASS

Engraving on glass has traditionally been left in the hands of professionals. However, a system of engraving with an electric vibrator tool has been developed that is so simple, the amateur can produce marvellous results easily. Your hardware dealer or craft supply house carries these engravers. They are generally equipped with a point of tungsten carbide, and some manufacturers also make a diamond point that is interchangeable with it. A common rate of vibration is about 7200 strokes per minute, and some are adjustable, so that the length of stroke can be varied to engrave a light line or a heavy one. In principle, the instrument can be compared to a pneumatic drill in miniature.

When the point is drawn across the surface, it leaves behind a great number of fine, tiny holes in the glass. As these run together, the result is a line.

The only difficulty is that because glass is so slick, the instrument tends to slip on it, particularly when you are engraving a dish on the concave inside, or a drinking glass with a convex surface. When engraving with the electric engraver, you must be sure to wear goggles or a plastic face-shield, because the action of the point flings minuscule splinters

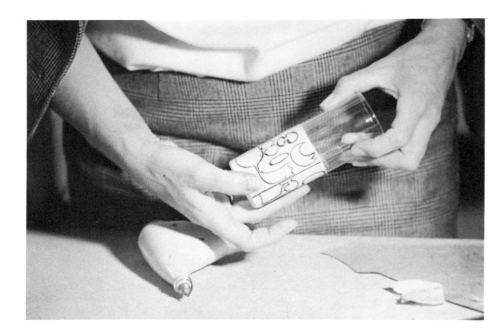

Illus. 101. Draw your design on very thin paper measured to fit the glass you intend to engrave.

of glass in all directions and with considerable force. The danger of getting such glass splinters in your eyes is a very real one.

Both problems can be solved by sticking on a piece of transparent, gummed tape over the area to be engraved. The point then has less tendency to slip and the glass splinters are in large measure kept under control by the gummed tape.

To start, draw a design on very thin paper or fabric and tape it down where you want the engraving. The engraver will easily engrave through both layers—tape and paper. This works particularly well when you are using an adjustable engraver, as you can adjust the

Illus. 102. Then tape the design to the glass.

86

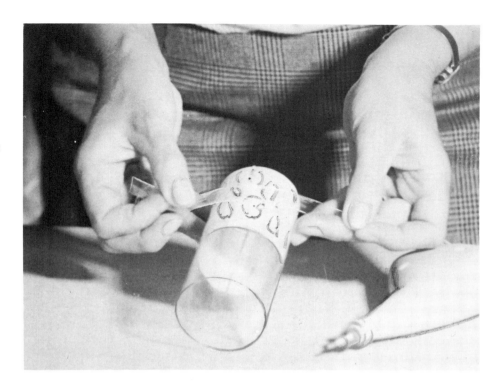

Illus. 103. Completely cover the design with the gummed tape.

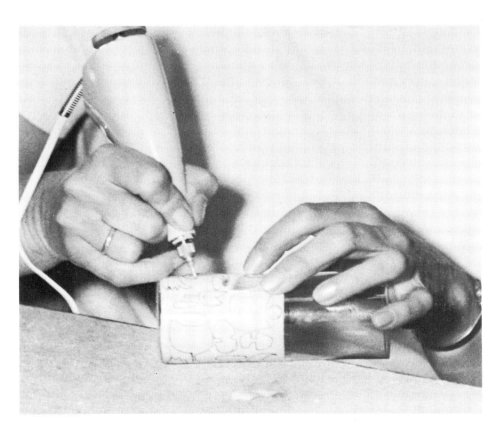

Illus. 104. Engrave the glass right through the tape and paper.

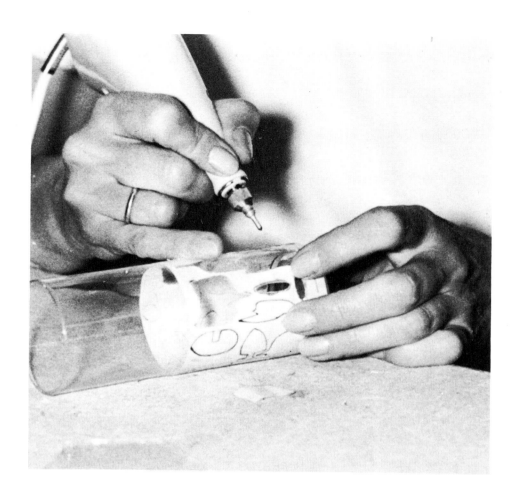

length of stroke to strike deeper when punching through the covering. A little practice at adjusting the stroke will soon tell you how much force is needed to penetrate both layers.

A simple method is to paint a thick glass blank with Glas-O-Past-X and shape it in the kiln into a dish. Then you can stick the design you have created wherever you please on it and engrave it into the glass. The plain glass exposed thus forms the design, standing out white against the colored background.

Also, you can engrave an existing dish, vase, or drinking glass with Glas-O-Past-X and fire it at a low temperature. For example, at about 1202° F. (650° C.)—cone 020, the glass will not be deformed, but will acquire a better light refraction. This will greatly enhance its appearance.

Another possibility is engraving plain drinking glasses, or, you might color the outside of the drinking glasses first with transparent Glas-O-Past-X before engraving. First, apply a thin coat of paint and let it dry thoroughly. This will serve as a base for a second, thin coat. The second coat does not have to be dry and the glass can be exposed to heat directly.

If the color is not smooth enough, a third coat can be added. Remember, two or three coats of thin paint provide a more even color than one heavy coat.

Do not heat the glasses higher than 1121°–1202° F. (605°–650° C.)—cone 022–020. Higher

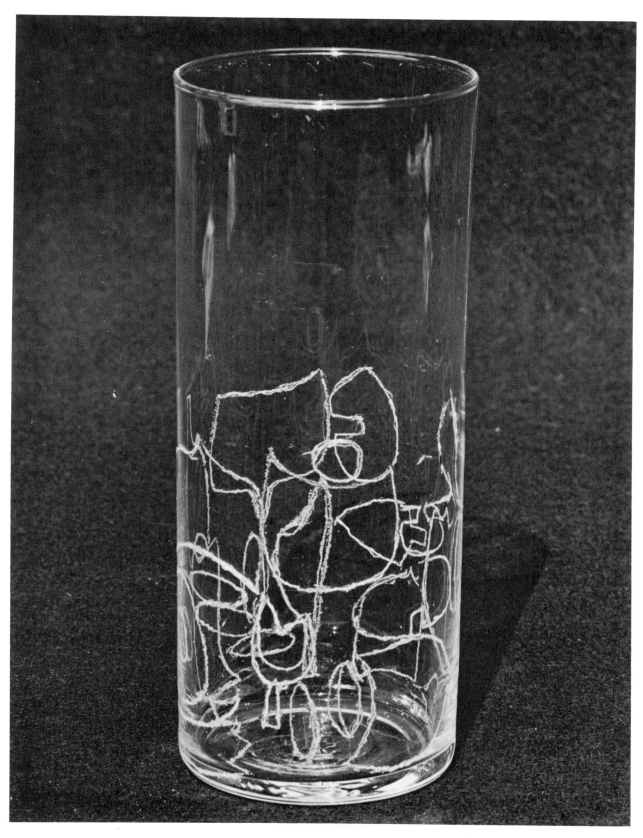

Illus. 106. The finished engraving.

heat will deform the shapes of drinking glasses. Then, the gleamingly colored glasses can be engraved. Wherever the engraver touches, the color is also removed. When choosing your colors, always take into consideration the function of the glasses. For example, white wine can be poured into green or blue glasses, but red wine and fruit juices lose their attractive look in glasses of those colors.

Still another way to decorate is to give the glasses a coating of color on the inside. Pour transparent Glas-O-Past-X thinned only with acetone into a glass. Then pour it out while rotating the glass, in the same way that you apply a coating of separator to a forming dish. There is one important difference, however, in that the latter is applied to a porous surface and therefore clings quite readily. This does not happen when Glas-O-Past-X is applied in this manner to a slick surface. So, you must thin the paint with nothing more than acetone and, after the paint has been poured out, you must keep on rotating the glass until the acetone has evaporated. If you don't do this, the paint will sag to the bottom.

Also, you should apply a number of thin coats, one over the other, allowing each to dry. If the coating is too thin, the result will be a fuzzy look. Place the glasses on a prepared kiln shelf and heat the kiln to 1121°–1202° F. (605°–650° C.)—cones 022–020. Let cool thoroughly. Proceed to engrave the glass. You will find that the result is entirely different from that achieved when the color is on the outside of the glass. There is less contrast, and the decoration is more subtle.

Color only the foot of long-stemmed wine glasses for another effect, or decorate the foot with mosaic glass. For this, use small bottle gems. Lay them on the foot of the glasses, place in the kiln and heat to 1121°–1202° F. (605°–650° C.)—cones 022–020.

Checklist for Engraving Glass:
Select a glass test plate and lay a piece of thin paper on it. Stick this down with transparent, gummed tape. With an electric engraving tool, write your name on the glass. Hold the engraver in a vertical position while using.
Check to see if the point has penetrated both layers and contacted the glass. If not, set the engraver control for a heavier stroke and check again.
Measure the circumference of a cylindrical vase or a glass.
Cut out a piece of thin paper of the same size. Draw a simple design on it.

Wrap the paper tightly around the glass. Stick it down with transparent tape.
Pick up the electric engraver and hold it in a vertical position. Trace slowly over the lines of the drawing. *Be sure to wear goggles or a plastic face-shield.*
Hold small glasses in your hand; lay large vases and dishes on a cloth on a table, or use a double thickness of corrugated cardboard.
Be careful with thin glass, as you might engrave right through it. Keep the engraver constantly moving, and never let it rest on one spot.
Remove the remains of the paper and transparent tape. Wash the glass with detergent.

BOTTLE

CUTTING

Illus. 107. An ordinary mustard jar, minus its neck, colored with transparent Glas-O-Past-X and heated to a deforming temperature.

Ordinary bottles of all kinds can be transformed into vases, drinking glasses, compote jars or whatever use your imagination dictates simply by removing the necks. In addition, the "unwanted" necks provide valuable material for your glasscrafting.

While there are several methods of removing the necks, the simplest and cleanest method of all is with a bottle cutter that has gained tremendous popularity recently. It consists of a device that comes fully assembled and which makes a scored line around the bottle wherever desired, and then breaks the glass along the score by a tapping from the inside.

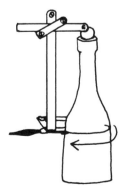

Illus. 108. A commercial bottle cutter.

No heat, no water, no mess. This inexpensive device comes complete with printed directions and is available at hobby shops and craft supply houses. Many hardware dealers also carry it.

However, you can manage very well with nothing more than a length of wool knitting yarn, a bottle of denatured alcohol and a bucket of cold water.

Remove all labels from the bottle, as well as the glue that held them on. Clean the bottle thoroughly on the outside. Watch out you do not get water inside the bottle, and never try to cut the neck off a wet bottle. It will simply not work as well as when the bottle is dry.

First, put on your goggles or shield. Saturate the piece of wool yarn with denatured alcohol, then wrap it round the straight part of the bottle, just below the shoulder. (Do not

Illus. 110. Set the yarn on fire immediately.

92

Illus. 111. When the alcohol is almost burned away, drop the bottle into a bucket of cold water.

try to use a cotton string for this. It just won't work.) Before the alcohol has a chance to evaporate, touch a match to the yarn.

When the alcohol is almost burned out, thrust the bottle quickly in water. As a result of the tension induced in the glass by heating and the sudden change of temperature, the neck of the bottle will crack off, precisely at the place where the yarn touched the glass, with a loud cracking sound. It is important to wrap the yarn horizontally round the bottle, not on an angle.

If your first attempt is not successful, try it with another bottle. The first bottle then gets a chance to cool off and dry.

Generally, the neck seldom springs from the bottle, leaving a precisely square break

Illus. 112. The quick change in temperature should cause the neck to snap off with a loud noise.

behind. But, the more bottles you try, the more skill you acquire, and, in time, you will have better results.

After separation, the edges of the glass will be quite sharp. File them smooth with a fine carborundum stone, and you will have a lovely cylindrical vase. If you cut the top of the bottle off fairly low down, use it as a compote bowl. Clean it on the inside with a good detergent or other strong cleanser, until the glass sparkles. Use the cracked-off neck when you make a wall collage (see page 46).

There is another method of "cutting" the neck off a bottle, which is, however, not as satisfactory, but you should be familiar with it. In this method, fill the bottle with oil to the line where you desire the break to come. Next, thrust a red-hot metal rod through the neck of the bottle, deep into the oil. The oil heats up along the rod, climbs upward, and forms a glowing hot layer on the surface. At this point, dip the bottle in cold water. Theoretically, the neck will snap off with a faultless break. In practice, however, it is not foolproof. Moreover, the oil gives off a terrible odor and you will have a miserable mess of oil spots to clean up afterwards.

When you have become skilled at cutting the necks off bottles, select a number of colorless glass bottles and make some cylindrical vases out of them. Coat the insides of the vases with a mixture of transparent-colored and white Glas-O-Past-X. Do not add paint thinner to the paint, only acetone, and keep the bottle turning until the last of the acetone has evaporated. Repeat this once more. Heat the vases to about 1121° F. (605° C.)—cone 022.

Checklist for Cutting off Bottle Necks:
1. Cutting bottles with a bottle cutter: Remove label and glue, and clean the outside of the bottle thoroughly. Oil the glass-cutter wheel with kerosene, sewing-machine oil, or similar lubricant. Place the device in position on the neck of the bottle. Wear goggles or a plastic face-shield. Set the cutter accurately. Check the alignment. Make one light, just-audible cut in one continuous turn. Follow the complete directions that come with the cutter.
2. Remove the label and glue from the bottle. Clean the bottle on the outside, but take care that the inside stays dry. Soak a piece of wool yarn in

alcohol. Wrap it as tightly as possible around the bottle, tie it, and snip the ends off short. Set fire to it. When the alcohol is practically burned out, stick the bottle in cold water. File the glass smooth along the edges with a fine carborundum stone. Wash the vase with detergent, inside and out.

3. Remove label and glue from the bottle. Pour oil in the bottle, up to the break-line. Heat an iron rod red-hot. Stick the glowing rod through the neck of the bottle, deep into the oil. Wait a few moments; then dunk the bottle in a bucket of cold water. Pour the oil out of the bottle. Clean the oil from inside the bottle. Rinse with alcohol. File the sharp edges smooth with a fine carborundum stone.

Illus. 114. Two bottle vases. The edges of the glass along the break will be sharp. File them with a carborundum stone until smooth.

BORING HOLES IN GLASS

When you use a single, thick plate of glass for a wall plaque or other hanging object, rather than a glass sandwich enclosing hanger-eyes, you will have to bore holes through the glass.

There are only a few things you must remember about boring holes through glass. One of these, and the most important, is: You can drill glass *only* with a hand drill. An electric drill turns too fast and heats up the glass, so that before you get too far along, the whole thing will crack. By the same token, you must not apply too much pressure. You only wear out the drill unnecessarily; you drill no faster than when you apply only a light pressure; and the glass is put under such strain that it will surely crack. Moreover, at the start of drilling, too much pressure will keep the bit sliding away from the place where you want to drill.

You can buy special drill bits for drilling through glass at practically any hardware dealer's. The bits are rather costly, but they last a very long time.

Slipping and sliding at the start of drilling is always a problem. If you have an electric engraver, you can engrave a little depression in the glass that will restrain the drill bit. Without an engraver, the task is a little more difficult; however, necessity is the mother of invention and you will soon find a method that works for you. For example, the diamond point of a grinding-wheel dresser can be usefully employed to scratch the glass for this purpose. Or, you can place the point of a carborundum stone against the glass and twist it and turn it in such a way as to roughen the glass just enough to keep the drill bit from sliding. The diamond point is better for this, of course, as the rubbing soon wears out the point on a carborundum stone, which has a total of only eight corners on the square stone, four at each end. However, you won't be drilling holes through glass every day.

Also roughen a place on the reverse side of the glass, directly in line with the rough spot on the face, for the glass has to be drilled from both sides towards the middle. Should you drill exclusively from one side, as the drill breaks through on the last part of the bore, the lips will catch, shattering and spoiling the glass around the hole, perhaps even cracking the piece. So, when a little way through the glass, turn it over and drill from the other side. Continue drilling a little and turning over until you have bored through completely.

When drilling, always lay the glass on a springy support. A double layer of corrugated cardboard or a thin layer of plastic foam is excellent for this. A thick layer of old newspapers will also serve.

Be sure to have a small bottle of paint thinner on hand. The paint thinner, or kerosene (paraffin), is used as a lubricant and coolant. Best, pour a little into a small dish and apply it to the drill bit from time to time with a brush.

Checklist for Boring Holes in Glass:
File the edges of the glass to be bored. Clean thoroughly with alcohol. Lay the glass plate on a piece of Masonite covered with two thicknesses of corrugated cardboard.

With the electric engraver, the diamond point of a wheel dresser, or the corner of a carborundum stone, make a rough spot on the glass.
Make a second rough spot directly opposite the

first one, on the reverse side. Brush a little paint thinner (or kerosene) on the rough spots.

Set the drill on the glass. Turn the drill at a slow, steady rate until a small pit has been bored into the glass. Brush again with thinner. Bore further. Turn the glass over and brush on a little thinner.

Set the drill in the rough spot and turn it carefully and steadily. Brush on a little thinner and continue drilling.

Turn the glass plate over. Continue in this way, drilling first from one side, then from the other, a little bit at a time, until a small opening has been made in the glass. Brush thinner on the drill bit so that it will run down into the hole as you drill.

Keep turning the plate over and back.

If you have not located the two bores directly opposite each other on both sides of the glass, the final breakthrough will not be precisely round, so that the glass plate will grab and turn with the drill. Get help from someone to hold the plate, or hold it down with a C-clamp. Put a piece of wood between the clamp and the glass and do not over-tighten. Once you have the glass held securely, carefully and without pressure, drill the hole out until it is round.

Bore the hole out enough so that the drill bit can be thrust all the way through the glass.

Make a Glass Candleholder

Now that you have learned how to bore holes in glass, try making a candleholder. You will need a round, glass plate about 5″ in diameter, a small copper dish such as used in enamelling, and a candle-pin (a sharp point that sticks into the bottom of the candle and holds it fast).

Drill a hole precisely in the middle of the glass plate and decorate the plate with Glas-O-Past-X. In this case, use only the single sheet of glass.

Next, lay the decorated plate on a prepared forming dish and heat in the kiln until the glass sags into the shape of the dish.

The hole in the glass plate will remain open throughout the shaping. Bore a similar hole in the middle of the small, copper dish.

Now, assemble the candleholder by placing the glass and copper dishes bottom-to-bottom. Pass the threaded end of the candle-pin through the hole in each, and turn the nut down tight. Your candleholder should look similar to the one in Illus. 115 (bottom right).

Illus. 115. By boring a hole in the glass, you can make a candleholder such as shown here at the bottom right.

Illus. 116. Glass from a shattered green bottle and from a jam jar colored with transparent blue Glas-O-Past-X was here combined with earthenware and fired.

GLASS COMBINED WITH EARTHENWARE

A Relief

A relief such as in Illus. 116 is a good way to experiment with this technique. Make the tile out of clay mixed with coarse grog. The best color for this purpose is the kind that burns black.

The thickness of the tile, or relief, must be at least 1″ to 1¼″, as the glass exerts very heavy pressure on it. In making a tile, always flatten and spread the clay out by patting it with your hands. Never use any kind of rolling pin, as if you were making biscuits. A rolled-out tile tends to become deformed, either while drying or in the kiln.

Use a heavy needle, not a knife, to cut out the openings in the tile. Clay will stick to a knife blade and make it difficult for you to keep the edges of the openings smooth.

The relief in Illus. 116 is made as follows: Press out flat with your palm a large lump of black-burning grogged clay mixed with black-baked grog to a flat disk. Then lay it on a piece of plastic. Scratch a design lightly into the clay with a needle.

Where the clay is to be worked up in relief, scratch in double lines. Cut out the openings with a needle and smooth the edges and the vertical sides of the openings to make them as smooth as possible. Pick up the tile by means of the plastic under it and turn it over. Smooth and round the edges of the openings at the back side of the tile. Near the upper edge of the tile, make an upward-slanting hole at least ¼″ deep. This hole will be used for hanging the tile on the wall.

Lay the tile on the flat surface of a plaster of Paris slab, face-side up. The relief work is applied to the tile in the form of little rolls of clay. Using the rounded end of a clay modelling tool, depress the space between the twin scratched lines a little, roughen it, then dampen slightly with a sponge or small sable brush. Apply a bit of slip. Apply the rolls of clay and smooth out the joints, then create the texture on the tile with the toothed end of a clay-modelling tool. When you are satisfied with the design, put the tile away, still on its plaster slab, to dry, and let it become leather-hard.

Now, to keep the tile from warping, lay a second plaster slab on top of the tile. Both slabs of plaster must be absolutely flat, and if you made them by pouring plaster of Paris into a rectangular wood form weighted down and resting on a sheet of glass, they are bound to be perfectly flat on the side that hardens against the glass. Make sure these are the sides touching the tile. Leave the clay between the slabs until it is completely dry.

The time required for the clay to dry depends entirely on the relative humidity of the atmosphere. During the winter, with furnaces going, the clay will dry considerably faster than during a moist summer. In general, you can expect it to take two or three weeks. When you are sure the piece is dry (hold it against your cheek), fire it in a kiln to biscuit temperature.

When the piece has cooled off, apply a transparent, ceramic glaze to the *vertical* sides of the openings. Do not let any glaze get on the face of the tile. Fire the glazed piece to the maturing temperature of both clay and glaze.

For filling the openings you need crushed glass. You cannot use glass gems; such fragments are far too big. Neither can you simply hammer the glass into bits, because, if you try this, you will wind up with nothing but powdered glass, interspersed with sharp-pointed chunks.

A very simple method for making glass grit is as follows: Take an ordinary, colored glass bottle and lay it on a separator-coated shelf in the kiln. Close the kiln and heat it quickly to about 932°–1112° F. (500°–600° C.). Cone 022 bends at 1121° F. (605° C.). This is the lowest-temperature cone available. Lower temperatures require a pyrometer to read them, or good judgment of the color of the kiln walls, which are just starting to glow. Shut off the kiln and immediately open it. With a pair of long-handled tongs lift out the hot bottle and drop it into a bucket of cold water. All at once, equally spaced, hairline cracks will spread over the entire surface.

If you then wrap the bottle in a cloth, you need only tap it a few times with the ball side of the hammer and the entire bottle will shatter into bits, all of approximately the same size, and there will be neither glass powder nor large fragments present. Of course, using colored bottles limits you in your choice of colors. You can, however, have grit of any color desired by coloring jars with Glas-O-Past-X.

Take a number of jam jars and clean them thoroughly with alcohol. Then squeeze $\frac{1}{4}$ to $\frac{1}{2}$ a tube of Glas-O-Past-X into a jam jar and stir in acetone to dilute and liquefy it. Tilt the jar over and turn it between your hands, so that the fluid paint coats the inside. Keep the jar turning for a few minutes as, since acetone evaporates quickly, the coating of paint quickly grows thicker and sticks to the inside of the jam jar. The more Glas-O-Past-X you use, the more intense is the resulting color. Do the same thing in other jars using different colors of Glas-O-Past-X, but avoid the colors that can be supplied by glass bottles.

Put the jam jars in the kiln and give them the same treatment described above for the bottle. Don't mix the different colors of glass grit—store each color in a separate jar. You will then have a good supply of colored, crushed glass. The example in Illus. 116 was made by using glass from a shattered green bottle and from a jam jar colored with transparent blue Glas-O-Past-X.

With the glass grit ready for use, lay the tile on a separator-covered kiln shelf. You will be able to see the kiln shelf, of course, through the openings cut in the tile. Apply a thin layer of dry, powdery separator in the openings of the tile. Take care to get none of the powder on unglazed parts of the piece. Any kind of powder is difficult to remove from unglazed clay and, if it is left on, it makes a dull, dun-colored splotch. Press the powder down firmly in the bottom of the openings with the tip of your index finger.

Use a teaspoon to fill up the openings in the tile with colorless crushed glass to $\frac{1}{8}''$. Then fill the openings with colored glass, but not to the top. Glass that is too thick is not as attractive as thinner glass, and it also exerts a far greater pressure, owing to expansion in the heat of the kiln, and too much can result in cracking the tile. A layer about $\frac{1}{4}''$ to $\frac{3}{8}''$ thick is quite enough.

Heat the tile to the usual temperature, and at that point, inspect the tile closely through the peep-hole to ascertain whether the glass grit has started to round off a bit. If it has not, it means that the glass is not yet sticking to the walls of the openings, so let the kiln continue to heat until it does; then shut it down. Make note of how far beyond the usual temperature you had to go for a thorough rounding of the glass, as an aid in doing future work. Give the piece 48 hours from the time of shutting down the kiln to become thoroughly cold.

Checklist for Melting Glass into Earthenware:
1. Lay a sheet of plastic on a table.
Take a lump of clay well-mixed with coarse grog and press it flat with your hands.
Form the desired tile-shape and cut off excess clay with a needle.
Scratch the design lightly into the soft clay.
Cut out the design with a needle.
Round off the edges of the openings and rub smooth the vertical sides.
Slip one hand under the plastic and turn the tile over.
Make the edges of the openings nice and round on the underside.
Make a sloping groove in the back side of the clay, near the top, for hanging it up.
Remove the plastic and lay the piece on a plaster slab, face-side up.
Roughen the space between the twin lines delineating the relief.
Dampen the clay a very little, add some slip, and lay rolls of clay in place.
Work the clay firmly to cause it to merge with the clay of the tile. Smooth out the seams where the two come together.
Texture the clay with the toothed end of the modelling tool. Let it get leather-hard.
Lay a second plaster slab on top of the piece and leave it until *thoroughly dry.*
Fire to biscuit temperature. Let cool.
Apply transparent glaze to the vertical sides of the openings.

Fire the piece again to the maturing point of both clay and glaze.
2. Lay a colored bottle on a prepared kiln shelf. Heat the kiln to 932°–1112° F. (500°–600° C.). Take the bottle out of the kiln with tongs and drop it into a bucket of cold water. Dry the bottle and wrap it in a cloth.
Strike the bottle (through the cloth) with the ball side of a hammer.
Open up the cloth and pour the crushed glass into a jar for storing.
3. Clean some empty jam jars thoroughly with alcohol.
Squeeze out some transparent, colored Glas-O-Past-X into a jar.
Dilute the paint with acetone and stir.
Turn the jar in your hands so that the paint runs all over inside, coating the glass. Keep turning until the acetone evaporates and the paint becomes so thick that it adheres to the glass.
Do the same with other colors of Glas-O-Past-X in the other jam jars.
Place the jars in the kiln and heat to 1121° F. (605° C.)—cone 022.
Take the hot jars out of the kiln with tongs and drop them into a bucket of cold water, and so on.
4. Lay the tile on a separator-painted kiln shelf.
Fill the bottoms of the openings very carefully with dry separator.
Press this down with the tip of your index finger and remove, with a small brush, any spills that happen to have occurred.

Fill the openings in the tile with about $\frac{1}{8}$-inch of colorless crushed glass; then fill up with colored glass to a total thickness of $\frac{3}{8}''$. Heat the tile to 1463° F. (795° C.)—cone 016.

Look through the peep-hole to see if the crushed glass is rounding off at the edges. If not, stand watch at the peep-hole until it does, then shut down the kiln.

Let the kiln cool off for 48 hours before opening.

Illus. 117. An unusual earthenware box with a glass-decorated top.

An Earthenware Box with a Glass Top

You can make a very attractive small box by decorating the cover with glass. First, cut a square out of a flattened piece of clay; then mark out the size of the bottom precisely in the middle. Cut squares out of the corners, so that you have a cruciform pancake of clay. Then fold the sides upwards along the edges of the bottom and mould the clay together at the corners. The result will be a square box. You can make a box like this one in a mould, pouring liquid clay in it.

Out of another square piece of clay make a cover for the box, adding an inside rim that fits easily into the box. In the middle of this square cover, cut a perfectly round hole. Then dry the box and top and fire. After firing, glaze the box with a ceramic glaze. However, make sure that the *inside* of the top, within the inner rim, remains free of glaze. The inner rim itself, of course, can be glazed.

After firing the glaze, set the box aside. Cut a round, glass plate just big enough to fit inside the inner rim on the underside of the earthenware top *without touching it*, and decorate with Glas-O-Past-X. Apply an even coat of separator to the unglazed surface inside the cover. Next place two strip-form kiln shelves in the kiln, some distance apart, each resting

Illus. 118. The hole was cut in the box before biscuit firing.

Illus. 119. The inside of the box has been glazed, but not the inside of the cover.

Illus. 120. Coat the inside of the cover with separator.

Illus. 121. A round plate of glass painted with Glas-O-Past-X is placed over the opening and the cover placed on shelf strips.

on two shelf supports. Then, lay the decorated glass plate exactly over the opening in the cover, with the uncolored side resting on the separator-protected surface. Then, place a star-stilt (a firing support for glazed ware) on each shelf strip, and place the cover upside down on the stilts. The hole in the top is thus clear of any obstruction (Illus. 121).

Heat the kiln until it begins to glow with a good color; then take your post in front of the peep-hole and keep a close watch on the action inside.

At the start of the bending temperature range, the glass, as a result of its own weight, will begin to bulge through the hole in the cover. When the bulge is well developed, shut down the kiln.

Take care that you do not let the glass bulge out too far, as the strain would be too great and the glass would crack. Let the kiln cool slowly.

After cooling, let the separator loosen itself from the underside of the cover. You will see that the glass has stuck to the vertical edges of the circular cut-out. If it doesn't do this— and this happens if the cover is very thin—glue the glass to the cover.

Checklist for Making a Box with a Glass Top:

Roll clay out thin on wrapping paper. Mark out a square in the middle of the clay.

Cut out the four corners so that a cross-shape results.

Fold the cut-out sides upwards and bond the corners to make a box by setting a small roll of clay between the two sides.

Make a little cover out of a flat piece of clay. Mould an inside rim on it.

Make a circular opening in the clay, say about $1\frac{1}{2}''$ in diameter for a cover $3\frac{1}{4}''$ square. Work the opening smooth. Let the clay dry thoroughly.

Fire the clay to about 1688° F. (920° C.)—between cones 010 and 09.

Glaze the box white on the inside and any color you please on the outside, but leave the inside of the cover unglazed.

Fire to the maturing point of both clay and glaze.

Coat the inside of the cover with separator.

Color a round, glass blank with Glas-O-Past-X, preferably transparent.

Lay the glass blank with the unpainted side against the inside of the cover.

Cover the points of two new star-stilts with a thin coat of separator.

Lay two narrow strips of kiln shelf on shelf supports. Lay a star-stilt on each strip. Span the space between the strip kiln shelves with the cover, so that it rests on both stilts with the opening clear of any obstruction and the glass can bulge out through it freely when heated.

Heat the kiln until the walls glow dark red; then watch the softening process through the peep-hole. Shut off the kiln when the glass bulges $\frac{3}{8}''$ below the cover.

Let the kiln cool slowly.

103

Illus. 122. A ready-made concrete block becomes an art object with a glass inset.

GLASS IN CONCRETE

Ready-made, open-work cement blocks are manufactured with many different shapes of weight-saving openings. How to fill the openings with fired glass depends on their shape. The block in Illus. 122 has one square and four L-shaped openings. To begin with, measure the openings exactly. The best way is to lay the concrete block on a sheet of paper on a table. Then, with a sharp-pointed pencil, outline the openings on the paper, using the edges as a guide. Remove the block and place a double thickness of corrugated cardboard under the paper. Lay the uncolored glass on the paper and follow the lines visible through the glass with a glass cutter, taking care to stay $\frac{1}{4}''$ to $\frac{3}{8}''$ *inside* the lines. You will need two plates of glass for each required shape, since you are going to use sandwiched glass.

The glass is simple to prepare. After cutting, file and clean the glass thoroughly. Then apply several transparent colors of Glas-O-Past-X with a few accents of orange or red opaque color. Lay some crushed glass, mosaic glass or chips on the glass. Place the glass on a broad strip of copper screen which should be at least 2″ wider on all sides. Later on you will use this to fasten the glasswork in place with mortar. Lay the second plate over the

Illus. 123. Trace the openings onto a piece of paper.

colored one and on top of that lay a few pieces of mosaic glass in vivid colors. The grey of the concrete calls for strong constrast.

Now, if you are making "L" shapes lay a strip of glass as wide as the corner opening on the paper and lay a strip of copper screen horizontally over it (Illus. 124). Then lay another glass strip on at right angles to the first, the end of one covering the end of the other. This is the only way an L-shaped opening in the corner of a block can be easily filled with glass. It is quite difficult to cut such a shape out of glass, because the line always cracks beyond the score in the glass, making it practically impossible to cut lines that are perpendicular to each other.

Next, lay a wide strip of copper screen over both glass strips, taking care to slip the screen under the top glass at the corner (Illus. 125). Again, the screen must project beyond the glass. Next, color the screen with a coat of thinned, transparent color. Be sure that no paint can flow off the glass, as this will ruin both the glass and the kiln shelf. Now, color a third

Illus. 124. For the "L" shapes, lay a strip of glass on the pattern the same width as the opening with a piece of copper screen over it.

Illus. 125. Lay another glass strip in the other direction with part of it lying on top of the first. Again, cover with copper screening.

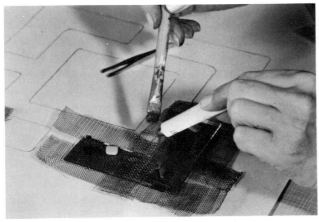

Illus. 126. Coloring the "L" shapes.

Illus. 127. The middle square. After firing, insert the various parts into the block and cement the screening to the block.

strip of glass and lay this horizontally upon the previous horizontal strip, with the colored side towards the screen.

Do the same with a fourth strip, which is placed vertically on the other pieces. The glass is now double everywhere except in the corner square, where it is quadrupled.

Repeat this procedure for all four corners of the block. Place the glass in the kiln and heat to 1454° F. (790° C.)—about cone 016. After cooling, insert the glass into the openings in the block with the screen bent towards the back. Secure the screen to the block with cement.

Checklist for Setting Glasswork in Concrete Blocks:

Lay the concrete block on wrapping paper. With a pencil, draw the shape of the openings on the paper, using their edges as a guide.

Set the block aside and draw new lines $\frac{1}{4}''$ inside the original lines.

Lay the paper on a double thickness of corrugated cardboard. Lay glass on the paper and cut it to size, using the inner lines to guide the cutter.

Cut glass in strips the width of the corner opening, four for each corner. File and clean the glass in the usual way. Decorate the middle panel with glass paint and transparent mosaic glass.

Lay a wide strip of copper screen along the edges of the glass, projecting 2″ beyond the edge.

Lay on a second glass plate and place the assembly on a prepared kiln shelf. Place a few pieces of transparent mosaic pieces in the middle of the glass.

Cut an L-shaped corner out of the paper pattern for a guide, and lay it on the kiln shelf. Place a strip of corner glass on it, and lay a strip of copper screen on top of that.

Lay on a second strip, horizontally, at right angles to the first, congruent in the corners. Color the screen with unthinned, transparent Glas-O-Past-X, but keep the paint inside the edges of the glass.

Color another strip of glass and lay it with the uncolored side on the screen.

Color still another strip of glass and lay it on the other side.

The glass is now double everywhere except in the corner, where it is quadrupled.

Heat the glass to 1454° F. (790° C.)—about cone 016.

Let the glass cool slowly. Take it out of the kiln. Bend the screen towards the back and slip the glasswork into the openings in the block. Cement the screen in.

EXPERIMENTING WITH COLOR

So far, your glass coloring has been restricted to Glas-O-Past-X. However, you will certainly want to experiment with other coloring techniques.

There are certain qualifications that must be fulfilled by a good glass-coloring medium that can be used at high temperatures. First to be considered is the coefficient of expansion. The glass you work with has an alkaline composition, and one of the main properties of alkalies is that they expand enormously with heat when combined with quartz. In addition, on cooling, there is also an exceptionally large percentage of shrinkage. The higher the firing temperature, the greater the expansion *and* the shrinkage. This requires a glass paint to have an especially wide range of adaptability and elasticity. If you know the precise chemical composition of the glass you are using and work only with that glass, then it is not so difficult to find a glass-coloring medium to fit it.

Compounding a glaze for earthenware involves the same thing. But every potter knows how difficult it is to adjust the coefficient of expansion of his glazes precisely to the kinds of clays he uses. If a glaze does not "fit" a clay, then hairline cracks appear in the glaze coating. The worst result of this is that a pot is thus made porous and will not hold water. Some kind of waterproofing medium then must be used.

However, if anything like this happens with glass, it cracks upon cooling and all your work will have been for nothing. The more different kinds and compositions of glass you use, the more likelihood of failures. Glass has a molecular alignment, something like the grain in paper or wood, which originates in the manufacturing process. If you lay two glass plates together, especially round ones, it is quite accidental if they happen to lie with their alignments parallel. Only a glass expert can detect this.

Glas-O-Past-X bridges over the difference in tension that is created between the two glass plates. That is why a coating of Glas-O-Past-X must be applied to all glass plates that have a second glass laid on top. This is necessary also wherever the use of color is not really needed, such as where parts of plants are enclosed between two pieces of glass. In such cases, a somewhat greater thinning of the paint is recommended.

Glas-O-Past-X is thus adapted to the coefficient of expansion of all kinds of glass and absorbs the differences in the stresses appearing in the glass.

In addition to Glas-O-Past-X, however, you can buy glas-dust, which is adjusted to the coefficient of expansion of most kinds of glass. It is completely colorless and transparent, and therefore you have plenty of room for experiment with it. Remember, every color oxide you add can change the coefficient of expansion, but not too much because glas-dust has a somewhat dissolving effect on an upper layer of glass. (Glas-dust is a silicate with a low melting or fusing temperature.)

With a fine sieve, sift the powder very thinly on the glass, creating a colorless adhesion between the two plates, or sprinkle a small quantity of color oxide or carbonate over the glas-dust between two pieces of glass. The powder can also be mixed with water and applied to the glass surface in a smooth, even coat. (Let the water dry out before firing, or steam created in the kiln will frost the glass.) Also, try mixing two, or even three, different oxides with the glas-dust. You will then get other results with many in-between tints that are well worth the effort. Such colors will be your very own, just as for the potter who compounds his own glazes which nobody can copy precisely.

Illus. 128. This painted dish is mounted on a wood base.

Some Ideas for Making Your Own Glass Colors

For each color, take about two ounces of glas-dust and dry-mix it in a small jar with any of the following:

1. A level teaspoonful of cobalt carbonate for transparent blue.
2. Half of the above for a light blue tint.
3. A level teaspoonful of copper carbonate for transparent light turquoise.
4. A little more for dark turquoise.
5. A level teaspoonful of chrome oxide for semi-transparent, dark green.
6. A half-teaspoonful of cobalt carbonate with a heaping teaspoonful of copper carbonate for Persian blue.
7. A half-teaspoonful of iron oxide for transparent yellow ochre.
8. A half-teaspoonful of nickel oxide for chartreuse.
9. A teaspoonful of manganese oxide for transparent, brownish purple.

By adding a level teaspoonful of tin oxide to the above mixtures, you can make the colors opaque. Tin oxide makes the glass colors elastic. A half-teaspoonful of tin oxide results in opalescent tints.

Cobalt- and copper-carbonate, and also manganese oxide, all have the property of lowering the melting point of the paint. The glass paint may also look as if it has boiled, showing craterlike formations. You can avoid this by adding two teaspoonfuls of an antiflux per teaspoonful of color oxide or color carbonate in the mixture. This is a silicate that raises the melting point and is, at the same time, adapted to the coefficient of expansion of glass.

All the materials can be mixed dry by shaking them up thoroughly in a jar with the lid on. (If tin oxide is added, it is advisable to rub the ingredients out on a piece of frosted glass with a palette knife.)

Using Ice Colors for Decorating

Ice colors are silica glass in a fine, granular form, mixed with a color. You may be familiar with its use in lamp shades. The shades are usually made of white milk glass, and the ice color is generally a golden yellow.

The surface of the glass is first covered with a thin coating of glass glue. The ice color is then sifted on through a nylon sieve, producing an even layer. You can do this yourself with milk glass lamps which you feel give off too cold a light. When you apply a coat of golden-yellow ice color over it, the quality of the light changes immediately to a warm, cheerful glow.

However, the importance of ice color in your work is the *texturing effect* which it provides when it is used with Glas-O-Past-X colors.

First, cut several round, glass blanks and file and smooth the edges as usual. Color the bottom plate with a transparent color of Glas-O-Past-X—try blue for the first test. At the same time, place two transparent colors, or a transparent color and black, together, painted one on top of the other, so you can see what happens when one color is painted over another. Then spread golden-yellow ice color over the surface—this time you do not have to pre-coat with glass glue. Just sift the color over the wet paint. Let it dry thoroughly. Next, lay the second uncolored glass blank on the prepared forming dish and place the colored glass plate, painted-side down, upon it.

Now heat the glass to bending temperature, that is, 1463° F. (795° C.)—cone 016. This results in a mixture of the colors and, where the yellow ice color was spread over the blue paint, a lovely green developed. However, because you sprinkled the surface stain around with a sieve, the color varies in all its inbetween tints towards blue. Moreover, an especially handsome-looking texture develops. The color is no longer even. The colorless, granular material forming the body of the ice color has created texture (see color page H).

Surface stain can also be used directly upon the glass, without applying any paint, which results in a rather dull-looking surface.

If you heat it to about 932° F. (500° C.), when the kiln is just beginning to glow with the dullest of dull red radiation, as is done with lamps and vases, it does not lose its granular texture. However, if you heat it to the temperature at which glass softens and you can shape dishes, then it is no longer visibly apparent that an ice color was used, insofar as the formation of texture and color changes are concerned. Ice colors are a great addition to decorated and fired glass.

Checklist for the Use of Surface Stain:
Cover a large light bulb with a very thin coat of glass glue.
Place a large piece of paper on the table and on top of that, a fine, nylon sieve.
Hold the light bulb over the paper and carefully sprinkle it with ice color, using the sieve. Set the lamp aside. Fold the paper together, and carefully pour the surplus ice color back into its jar.
Lay the light bulb on a prepared kiln shelf.
Heat the kiln to 932° F. (500° C.) to avoid deforming the glass.
Shut down the kiln and let the glass cool until all strains are released.

Checklist for Texture on Dishes:
Cut two glass plates, and file them smooth and round on both sides. Clean the glass and cover one plate with transparent blue Glas-O-Past-X.
With a broad, flat brush, give the plate a few quick brushes with black Glas-O-Past-X. Sprinkle the still-wet paint evenly with golden-yellow ice color. Let dry.
Lay the second glass plate on top and fire to 1463° F. (795° C.)—cone 016.

APPENDIX

Mistakes and How to Avoid Them

You can be ever so careful and skilful in working with glass, yet now and again a moment will arrive when you will ask yourself: What mistake did I make with this? The following are typical mistakes, and some ways to avoid them.

Cracks in flat plates lying directly on the kiln shelf

a. The temperature was raised too quickly in the kiln, so that the glass got hot more quickly than the kiln shelf. The thicker the kiln shelf, the slower the temperature must rise.

b. The temperature in the kiln was raised too quickly, so that the thin parts of the glass got hot more quickly than the thick fragments laid on it.

c. Cooling was forced by opening the door or cover of the kiln, so that the glass did not have time to fully relax the strains set up in it.

d. The glass was taken from the kiln while it was still hot, or lukewarm. Tension was still present in the glass, causing cracks to show up a few hours or a few days later.

It appears from the above that all cracks are a result of heating too fast or cooling off too fast.

Cracks in dishes

a. The kiln cooled off too quickly because the door or cover was opened, and the glass did not have time to fully relax its tension.

b. The glass was taken from the kiln hot or lukewarm.

c. The two glass plates were of differing composition.

d. The glass plate was larger in diameter than the forming dish.

Bulging of glass dishes

a. The forming dish was biscuit-fired at too high a temperature so that it was not porous enough to let the air escape from between the glass plate and the form.

b. The glass was over-heated.

c. The kiln temperature was raised too quickly.

d. The forming dish was used too wet.

Glass dishes with sharp, uneven edges

a. The glass plate was not filed completely smooth so that the sharp glass, when laid on or in the forming dish, cut through the coating of separator and the glass got hung up on the earthenware.

b. The Glas-O-Past-X was not removed from the edges.

The glass is spottily frosted on the back and bulging here and there

a. Overheating of the glass.

b. Overheating of the glass together with insufficient drying of the separator.

c. You forgot to apply a fresh coat of separator.

Bad color development

a. The Glas-O-Past-X was thinned too much.

b. The glass was heated too far beyond the softening point.

Over-heating of the glass when the temperature adjustment is correct

a. The kiln shelf or the kiln cover was less than 4" above the glasswork, so that after-radiation took place.

b. Your pyrometer needs checking and repairing.

110

Cracking-off of laid-on glass, such as mosaic glass
  a. You used window glass or show-window glass of a composition different from usual.
  b. You forgot to apply a coat of Glas-O-Past-X under the pieces.
  c. You forgot to apply a layer of glas-dust under them.
Total loss of color in the glass
  a. You used ordinary glass paints instead of Glas-O-Past-X.
Damage to the forming dish or kiln shelf
  a. You got Glas-O-Past-X on the edge or underside of the glass.
  b. The glass was heated too far above its softening point.

Firing Temperatures for Different Uses

These are all the cone numbers and temperatures you will have use for in glass shaping. As you may have noticed, certain results can be achieved at differing temperatures. You should keep a stock of all the differently numbered cones on hand. The most useful temperatures for glass shaping are from 1463°–1481° F. (795°–805° C.). If you get really "wrapped up" in glass shaping, it is a good idea to lay in a good supply of cones 016 and 015, and a smaller quantity of each of the others. Unless, of course, your kiln is equipped with an accurate pyrometer.

Standard and Junior Size Cones

Cone	Degrees Fahrenheit	Degrees Centigrade	Color of Kiln Interior	Use
022	1121	605		
021	1139	615		
020	1202	650		Liquid gold.
019	1220	660		Painting of vases, etc. Heating bottles for crushed glass.
018	1328	720	Dull	Light deforming of painted vases. Heavier deforming of glasswork.
017	1418	770		Melting in plant parts. Shaping dishes from very soft glass.
016	1463	795		Shaping dishes from normal window- and show-window glass.
015	1481	805	Red	Firing jewelry, plaques, collages, reliefs, etc.
014	1526	830		Firing clay for forming dishes.
013	1580	860		Firing clay for forming dishes.
012	1607	875	Cherry Red	
011	1643	895		Firing forming dishes with air escape holes.
010	1661	905		Ditto.
09	1706	930		Normal biscuit fire, glass gems.
08	1742	950	Orange	Gems from glass fragments.
07	1814	990		Glass gems. Glass mosaic in melted state.
06	1859	1015		
05	1904	1040		Glazing.
04	1940	1060	Yellow	Stoneware biscuit.
03	2039	1115		

INDEX